Ken Page's room & had a lovely tin
en we got to run Pekes with Ken
d – Chocolate Box   rour
e star trap. It   as if
e stage is vomiting   forth : one
the most astonishing effects I've
er seen. We got midway thru the
ll, falling short of Trevor's aim
going at least to the interval.
th after the break, Tim stayed
run his solo. He was marvelous,
it midway thru landed badly on
is left ankle. Everyone froze,
it he walked it off & continued
inishing superbly. Everyone cheered
e is a star dancer of the highest
egree. Many of his moves drew
asps, even from us who know he
Then he hurriedly put some ice on
the ankle.

  While I changed, the boat was
dropped in, including the wonderful

Published by
Smith and Kraus, Inc.
177 Lyme Road, Hanover, NH 03755
www.SmithKraus.com

Cover and Text Design by Freedom Hill Design, Reading, Vermont
Photos by Martha Swope/Timepix

Front cover photo: Stephen Mo Hanan as Gus the Theatre Cat
Back cover photo: Trevor Nunn surrounded by (clockwise from top)
Harry Groener (partially blocked), Wendy Edmead, Timothy Scott,
Steven Gelfer, Whitney Kershaw, Cynthia Onrubia,
Reed Jones, Bonnie Simmons, Janet Hubert,
René Clemente (partially blocked), Herman Sebek

First edition: November 2001
9 8 7 6 5 4 3 2 1

ISBN 1-57525-281-3

A Cat's Diary

HOW THE BROADWAY PRODUCTION OF CATS WAS BORN

Stephen Mo Hanan

ART OF THEATER SERIES

A Smith and Kraus Book

ACKNOWLEDGEMENTS

Proceeding instantaneously from A to Z, I want to thank Andy Zerman, whose casting acumen led me to *Cats* in the first place, and whose courage and persistence in the years since have been unfailing exemplary beacons.

Over lunch with the inner circle of *Jolson & Co.* in late summer of 2000, I mentioned (in view of the imminent closing) that I'd kept a diary of the original *Cats* rehearsals. Jay Berkow and Peter Larson, my collaborators, and Ric Wanetik, our producer, all dropped their forks and insisted that I find a place to print some excerpts to go along with the anticipated hoopla. Tom Chiodo, skilled publicist and faithful friend, sent a xerox copy of some handwritten pages to Robert Simonson at *Playbill,* who immediately wanted them for the *Playbill Online* web site and in his enthusiasm undertook to have them transcribed. My heartfelt thanks to them all for lighting up that spot hidden under my nose.

Many old friends from Telluride, Harvard, and Haight-Ashbury days have been stalwart pillars all along, and I would like to acknowledge in order of intelligence (no, just kidding) Ben Bayol, Judith Bruce, Julie Clark Boak, Cort Casady, Timothy Crouse, Howard Cutler, Robert Dawidoff, Emily DeHuff, Marlys Edwards, Kathy Frankovic, Peter Gabel, Bill Graustein, Jesse Kornbluth, Ed Kovachy, Richard Noll, Victoria Traube, and even John Weidman.

Because everybody who loves language teaches it, I thank Sara Peller, Gary Gomer, Jim Roman, Daniel Marcus, Janet Friedman, Freyda Thomas, Hal Glatzer, "Fox" Ellis, David Schwartz, Kathryn Walker, Mark Bennett, and Mudra.

And then there's Trevor.

Contents

Introduction
by Trevor Nunn

The New York production of *Cats* was the first work that I did in America, cast with American artists and followed through from first rehearsal to first night; it was a life-changing experience. I suspect this was as true for the many others involved, as the extraordinarily loyal, happy, and emotional reunions over the years has demonstrated, and as this book by Stephen Mo Hanan celebrates.

Raised as I was in a small industrial town in a somewhat remote area of England known as East Anglia, I first encountered Broadway musicals through the medium of film—*Oklahoma!, Carousel, South Pacific, The King and I*—and obsessed by all things theatrical as I was, it became imperceptibly my life's ambition to experience being a professional on the Great White Way. Every time I heard a throwaway reference—give my regards to Broadway, Broadway here I come—I received it as a reminder or a stimulus for my mission.

So although work of mine had already appeared in a Broadway season, when the RSC *Nicholas Nickleby* played a limited engagement at the Plymouth Theatre (and that's another story), the news that *Cats* had been assessed as worthy of becoming a Broadway show was a matter of joyous Superbowl celebration for me.

Cats had started in London without any such ambitions. Andrew Lloyd Webber, a restless seeker after new forms and untried approaches to musical drama, had shown me his ten settings of children's poems by the American-born poet T.S. Eliot (in my view indisputably the great poetic voice of the twentieth century in our language) and asked whether I thought it might be possible to make them the basis for a stage show. I was intrigued that Andrew should be embarking on something that was, in essence, an experiment, demanding and expressing a belief in pure theatre and shared imagination, but with no poles like plot or character development, or even at that stage considerations like time and place, to hold up the tent.

The work began in improvisation, and like all such projects requiring collective belief, there was more than one occasion when it threatened to collapse under the pressure of its own uncertainties. I remember telling the company in need of reassurance that what we were doing was no more preposterous than, for example, asking children to believe in Aladdin's magically opening cave, a genie in a lamp and a flying carpet—belief comes from the storyteller.

Our inventions of narrative and relationship had to be largely in the mind, unsupported by text, because Eliot had written 'occasional' verses with no intention that they should be linked together, and because the Eliot estate had insisted that only the words of Eliot could be uttered. But this circumscription led eventually to a willingness on the part of the actors to engage spiritually to explore how much of a 'sixth sense' could be reached and subtextually communicated.

All this is a very far cry from the more everyday pressures of putting on a musical, including the natural concerns each performer had for their "big moment," and the endless and necessary negotiation between music and dance departments both needing to satisfy their own demands of form and structure. And of course all these things went on by the bucket load, and with the gloves off. No, I don't mean to suggest that we all went about thinking we had achieved nirvana, and bowing to one another in reverence. We were as knockabout and nervous and venal as any theatre company anywhere. But we nonetheless realized that it was only by trusting to the power of the imagination that we would alchemies our material into something transfiguring, and that commitment remains our bond to this day.

My colleagues and I were still in a state of disbelief that our show should be so phenomenally successful in London, so we entertained no thoughts that success in New York would be a foregone conclusion. I don't think I have ever felt so superstitious about the casting process as I did putting together the New York company, trying to find the mysterious x-factor for each role, as much as evaluating skills with singing and acting and dancing.

Nobody has ever had more of that unquantifiable x-ingredient than Stephen Mo Hana. A passionate lover of language and all its attendant possibilities of imagery, wit, and multiple meanings, he is also a born master of impro-vised comedy and an individualist who believe more than anything else in ensemble. His optimism was a vital part of the process of this life-changing production and I recapture some essence of it every time I read his signature at the end of one of his letters, accompanied as always by "thrive and beam," the phrase that he has made his own. His book encapsulates everything of that time in the theatre, but even more it tells us about the remarkable generosity and human-ism of the writer.

AUTHOR'S NOTE

I played featured parts in two hit Broadway shows before I ever had an agent, a hint of the unconventionality that has marked my career and life. The transition from Harvard graduate to San Francisco street singer to Tony nominee seems unremarkable to me because I lived it, but my intrigued publisher thought it might call for some context. Of course the true context for anybody's life is everybody else's life (which is why theater matters), but I will try to condense my truth into the briefest form sufficient to introduce what follows.

The only child of Orthodox Jewish parents, I grew up in Washington, DC, fell in love with the theater at an early age, graduated with the Harvard Class of '68 and won a Fulbright Fellowship to study acting at the London Academy of Music and Dramatic Art. My return to America coincided exactly with what came to be known as Woodstock, and over the following year, as assaulting the competitive hierarchies of New York theater failed to nurture me, the cooperative and egalitarian values of the rising counterculture came to look better and better. By the spring of 1970 I was approaching a crisis of conscience, and its resolution took a radically unexpected form.

On a trip to Israel that April, I dropped mescaline on the Mount of Olives and had an overwhelming religious experience in the Garden of Gethsemane (they don't call it the Holy Land for nothing): fiery Hebrew letters, a feeling of prodigious joy, and an unshakable conviction that we are, every one of us, linked manifestations of a single sacred love source. About such experiences whole books could be written (and have), but for now suffice it to say that God hiccuped and my priorities shifted. Enflamed, like many of my contemporaries, by the vision of a culture less repressive and more heartfelt, I abandoned the commercial theater and took to singing on the street, mostly Italian opera. In Richard Nixon's Washington this seemed like a useful way to counteract the vibes, at least until I was busted by the musically challenged DC police. When a few months later on a visit to San Francisco I was handsomely paid for performing the very same repertoire for which in Washington I'd been arrested, I decided to relocate. I joined a Haight-Ashbury commune of like-minded flower adults, found a terrifically lucrative street-singing spot (the Sausalito Ferry Terminal), learned to accompany myself on the concertina (its squeezebox chords suited the arias), and kept at it for about six years. Near the end of that time the American Conservatory Theater produced a play I'd written, and its enthused reception led me once again to New York.

While Joseph Papp's New York Shakespeare Festival was considering my play (he ultimately passed), their casting director got wind of my singing and put me into one of the free productions at the Delacorte in Central Park, then another and then another. This last was *The Pirates of Penzance* with Linda Ronstadt and Kevin Kline, and the commercial transfer of that production occasioned my Broadway debut (with concertina) in 1981. I left *Pirates* after a year and on my first free night went to see another show where I encountered my friend Andy Zerman, who had just started work at Johnson-Liff Casting. Seeing that I was at liberty, he told me they were getting ready to cast a new Andrew Lloyd Webber musical that was a big hit in London, and there might be a part for me in it. Not only was he correct, but a sizable chunk of the part (the Growltiger sequence) was, as you shall read, specially created for me. Thus it transpired that in each of my first two Broadway shows I found myself on the deck of a pirate ship playing the concertina. Years later I faced a Broadway audience from yet a third pirate ship, but for Captain Hook (opposite Cathy Rigby), a concertina was out of the question.

I played the instrument at my very first *Cats* audition, astonishing both Trevor and Andrew though I didn't fully understand why till weeks later, when I learned that the original plan to make "Growltiger's Last Stand" a travesty of Grand Opera had been scrapped in London for lack of an actor with the requisite vocal chops. They were hoping to restore the concept for the Broadway production and when I launched into "Funiculi Funicula" (a Sausalito favorite), I appeared to be the answer to their prayers as much as they to mine. For my callback I was asked to prepare a passage of poetry that was theatrical. To me this was an almost blatant invitation to recite "The Ballad of Mighty Melvin," a mock-heroic piece I'd composed years before while waiting in line for standing room at the San Francisco Opera (see page 99). The risk was that its length was more than double the allotted three minutes, but I chanced it and was not only allowed to finish but greeted with rapture, especially by Trevor, who took me aside, inquired after the poem's source, and turned round to announce to everyone present, "And he wrote it!" Even so the role wasn't offered me until I'd passed (barely) two dance auditions for choreographer Gillian Lynne.

I first began to keep a journal in 1971 when, backpack above and bell-bottoms below, I hitchhiked across the country from Washington to San Francisco. The journey which culminated with the opening of *Cats* on Broadway in 1982 involved considerably less mileage, but was otherwise equal in discovery, inspiration, life lessons, and pleasure. Although at the time I had no thought of publishing (and was specifically forbidden by my director, as again you shall read), the impact of seeing Trevor Nunn's production of *Nicholas Nickleby* had been so great that I felt keeping an account of the *Cats* rehearsals was a good idea. He was obviously a director of genius and, as I learned during the audition process, one of enormous charm, humor, graciousness, and sound judgment. Qualities so rarely encountered seemed worth recording.

I never re-read the *Cats* journal until the show was on the verge of ending its record-breaking Broadway run in the late summer of 2000. At that point *Playbill Online* had expressed interest in putting some excerpts from it on their web site to honor the show's closing. One thing led to another, and now to my own amazement my diary is a book!

Because I wrote originally for no other eyes than my own, there are a number of references that will be meaningless to an outside reader and others that assume a level of familiarity with the story and background of *Cats* that not everyone will share, despite the general impression that it was seen at least once by every soul on Earth. I have therefore inserted footnotes from time to time to illuminate these more obscure corners of my experience. And I shall now withdraw to a corner myself to let an earlier me tell the story as it unfolded day by day nearly two decades ago.

Note about *Cats*

The text of *Cats* consists chiefly of Andrew Lloyd Webber's settings of poems from *Old Possum's Book of Practical Cats* by T.S. Eliot, with a modicum of linking material between the songs to create a story line, namely that once a year a tribe of cats called the Jellicles meets for a nocturnal Ball on an urban junk heap. At the end of the Ball the leader, Old Deuteronomy, selects one cat to ascend to the Heaviside Layer, undergoing thereby a magical exaltation. The various numbers represent each contender's bid to be chosen, an honor ultimately bestowed upon the outcast Grizabella.

CATS

THE ORIGINAL BROADWAY CAST

Music by Andrew Lloyd Webber
Based on *Old Possum's Book of Practical Cats* by T.S. Eliot

Presented by Cameron Mackintosh, The Really Useful Company
Limited, David Geffen and the Shubert Organization

Designed by John Napier
Lighting Design by David Hersey
Associate Director and Choreographer Gillian Lynne
(assistant Joanne Robinson, dance captain Bonnie Walker)
Directed by Trevor Nunn

Alonzo . . . . HECTOR JAIME MERCADO
Bustopher/Asparagus/Growltiger. . . . . STEPHEN HANAN
Bombalurina . . . . DONNA KING
Carbucketty. . . . . STEVEN GELFER
Cassandra . . . . RENÉ CEBALLOS (*girl-René*)
Coricopat/Mungojerrie . . . . RENÉ CLEMENTE(*boy-René*)
Demeter . . . . WENDY EDMEAD
Etcetera/Rumpleteazer . . . . CHRISTINE LANGNER
Grizabella . . . . BETTY BUCKLEY
Jellylorum/Griddlebone . . . . BONNIE SIMMONS
Jennyanydots . . . . ANNA McNEELY
Mistoffelees . . . . TIMOTHY SCOTT
Munkustrap. . . . . HARRY GROENER
Old Deuteronomy . . . . KEN PAGE
Plato/Macavity/Rumpus Cat . . . . KENNETH ARD
Pouncival. . . . . HERMAN W. SEBEK
Rum Tum Tugger. TERRENCE V. MANN
Sillabub . . . . WHITNEY KERSHAW
Skimbleshanks . . . . REED JONES
Tantomile. . . . . JANET L. HUBERT
Tumblebrutus . . . . ROBERT HOSHOUR
Victoria. . . . . CYNTHIA ONRUBIA
The Cats Chorus. . . . . WALTER CHARLES, SUSAN POWERS
CAROL RICHARDS, JOEL ROBERTSON
Swings . . . . Marlène Danielle, Diane Fratantoni,
Steven Hack, Bob Morrisey

A Reminder...

How soon hath Time, the subtle thief of youth,

Stolen on his wing my three and twentieth year!

My hasting days fly on with full career,

But my late Spring no bud or blossom showeth. . .

Yet be it less or more, or soon or slow,

It shall be still in strictest measure even

To that same lot, however mean or high,

Toward which Time leads me, and the will of Heaven.

All is—if I have grace to use it so—

As ever, in my great Task-Master's eye.

John Milton, Sonnet 7, 1632

Monday, 9 August 1982   DAY ONE

"First of all, would anyone who was able to sleep last night please raise their hand," are Trevor's first words, followed by: "And now anyone who isn't a rictus of nerves please do the same." Then, at the risk of seeming "hubristic" he goes round the circle introducing every actor and the role he/she is playing, thirty in all, including booth singers and swings, not stumbling until the very last one, a tall and strikingly beautiful black woman called Janet Hubert, whose character's name eludes him for a beat or two. "Just so you know I'm not perfect," he winks.

He fills the rest of the morning with the story of how CATS came to be: Andrew LW's home "Sydmonton festival" performance of the settings; the eventual decision to opt for a big theater piece rather than a chamber recital; the enlistment of Gillian and the whole choreographic concept; and the cooperation of Valerie Eliot, especially her discovery and offering of a wrinkled sheet of paper with four lines sketching "Grizabella the Glamour Cat." A long scholarly digression on T.S. Eliot (how many cast members make sense of "piling Pelion on Ossa," I wonder), and an often whispered but highly emotional reading of "The Naming of Cats" ending with his comment, "Now I propose that that is a serious poem."

Trevor is soft-spoken in the extreme, yet no one in the room seems to have any trouble hearing him. He exudes authority, gentleness, intelligence, commitment, interest. His flow of talk is precise, acute, and cultivated but without a trace of self-consciousness or self-importance. Speaking of the ensemble quality of the show (having already discussed at length certain key characters—including mine—"that old heart-breaker, Gus") he says, "You'll never hear me say that all the roles are of equal size. But I'll always, always insist that all the roles are of equal importance."

Pre-meeting scenes of recognition with Bonnie Simmons,[1] Anna McNeeley from Goodspeed, René Ceballos from her McCavity audition. (My first-day bake-offering, a peach custard torte, makes a big hit. Cameron Mackintosh asks if more desserts will be forthcoming and observes that the Britishers are especially fond of pecan pie.) Also I recognize Hector Mercado from *West Side Story*, Ken Page, Harry Groener, and Kenneth Ard from his acrobatics display at my last audition. Now sweeping the circle, I note the racial and ethnic diversity, the blacks, blondes, Hispanics, Asiatics, Semitics, et al. and the remarkable feline faces.

Andrew plays through major themes of the score. Quite a rush to hear him do "Memory." "Andre's Puccini ingredient," Trevor calls it, "the kind of melody that makes emotion

---

[1] My scene partner in "Gus," with whom I'd spent a year on Broadway in The Pirates of Penzance.

burst open too powerfully to be merely sentimental." We all sigh. Then we are led into an adjoining studio where chain-smoking, craggily handsome John Napier takes the brown paper wraps off the set model—the entire Winter Garden, four ft. square—and everyone gasps. A collage of the detritus (another Nunn word) of commercial civilization: discarded auto parts, bottle caps, broken phonographs, shredded magazines, old clothes, wrecked billboards, and everything spilling off the stage and into the house in so many directions that the proscenium is totally invisible. John shows off its little nooks and gimmicks like a ten-year-old with a railroad train set, taking special pride in the transformation that sets up the Growltiger scene (the back wall tilts down to display a full-size pirate ship built on the reverse side) and the apotheosis of Grizabella (Betty Buckley shows anxious concern about her climb up the stairway that descends from the ceiling and inquires—quite seriously—about insurance provisions in the event of permanent injury. John assures her that he always tries everything out himself.) Then the strip of brown paper that runs along two walls is taken down and Trevor invites us to inspect the "John Napier gallery." Oohs and ahs greet the mounted costume sketches. Even Bernie Jacobs[2] is smiling.

In the elevator at lunch break I meet Tim Scott, the Mr.

[2] President of the Shubert Organization, notoriously poker-faced.

Mistoffelees, and we head for Brownie's where the company table is full so we withdraw by ourselves. He has returned for this after five years in California, freelance dancing, lots of commercials. He tentatively refers to a religious teacher under whose influence he has come—a woman from San Diego—I mention Stewart Emory,[3] whose book Tim is reading, and boom! we're in the New Age. Of course, Tim had been suspecting it of me all morning (must have been the way I glowed—blushed?—when Andrew announced that I'd be singing a new Italian aria while playing the concertina!). He has also found spiritual kinship with Ken Page and René Ceballos—a full moon meditator. We wax rhapsodic over the opportunities the show presents for transformative effects—and for our own careers in that context—and both note that Trevor's spiritual qualities have not escaped us. An immediate bond, very open and loving eye contact.

We return to the small studio and meet Stanley Lebowski, the music director, a little roly-poly Sancho Panza, with a fascinatingly rabbinical manner: kindness and patience, wry humor mixed with a firm adherence to musical exactitude. We learn the harmonies of the opening number, everyone delighted to discover the group's full-blooded, well-balanced sound. Trevor announces that tomorrow, like every day

3 founder of the Actualizations awareness-training workshop & author of "You Don't Have to Rehearse to Be Yourself."

ahead, we'll begin with Gillian giving class; improvisation work will follow. After the usual Equity business, the day ends promptly at 6:30.

Tuesday 10 August Day 2

By 9:40 most of the cast is in the big studio warming up for class. Gillie comes in at 10:04 and off we go. Roundups, stretches, tendus, plié-relevés, flatbacks, battements, nothing I'm not prepared for,[4] apart from some unsteadiness balancing in relevé on one leg. Gillie is kindly and charming, lucid in her explanations and clarifications, and class is delightfully enhanced by the live piano of our accompanist, Kathy Summer, who inclines to jazzy renditions of Rodgers and Hammerstein. I feel confident by the end of class of my ability to cut it.

After a coffee break (friendships developing, alliances forming), we meet with Trevor for the first improvs. Everyone takes a partner and Trevor asks us, at the word "Go," to tell each other—simultaneously—some well-known fairy tale. We must speak and listen at the same time, and sure enough, at the end of that exercise we must—simultaneously—repeat the story we heard. Pandemonium. Switch

4 Not a trained dancer, I was hired 5 months before the start of rehearsals with the proviso that I take conscientious jazz & barre classes (at the producers' expense).

partners. I'm with Debbie, a tall, tigerish blonde. Now we do the same exercise, but making up our own story. Midway through, Debbie says, "I see what you're doing. You talk real slow and listen during the pauses." There's a "gotcha" in her tone that makes me uncomfortable—she's judging, not playing—but I persist. At the repeat, she can recount only one phrase from my story, while I tell a lot of hers. She gives me a "playful" push that expresses veiled resentment and I make a mental note to keep an eye on her.

Trevor draws us into circle again and gives a new assignment: pick a cartoon cat we know of, withdraw to ourselves and prepare a vignette of that cat, then return to circle and each in turn will present. (Subtext: our first chance to appear as individuals before the group.) I choose Fritz the Cat making a pass at some kitty. Watching the others is a gas—people's individualities are beginning to emerge: Harry Groener: lanky, goofy, gawkily limber as Sylvester, being whirled around by a passing train.

Whitney Kershaw: exquisite as a blonde Dresden doll, fresh-faced and eager, as Fifi the white cat, coquettish and pert.

Hector Mercado: grim-faced on Day One, now sly and subtle as Sylvester caught in the act of snatching Tweetie from her cage.

Ken Page: languidly debonair as the Pink Panther.

Then Trevor's probing, earnest questions: Who is Sylvester? Who is Tom (Tim Scott sneaking at top speed along a flattening wall)? Do they walk erect or on all fours?

Do they mix with humans or are they strictly feline? Why are cats such popular cartoon characters? Why are they so common? Mysterious? Aloof? Independent? What does it mean to be a "pet"? He is receptive to all ideas, while subtly guiding the discussion in the direction he wants, which is that of group discovery.

He asks us to pick a specific cat we know, and explore its consciousness: walking, then stretching, then cleaning, then all three. Add neutral alertness, fearful alertness, anger. No interactions yet. Back to circle. Why did nearly everyone end up on all fours? Discovery of different relationship to the floor, closeness of it, "neat stuff on it," the body parallel to it rather than perpendicular. But how to bring these discoveries into two-legged dancing?

Now we're to investigate a specific vignette of our cat that was amusing or endearing. Some amazing work ensues. Janet Hubert leaves the circle and tucks her long back frame against the window pane, trying to catch a bird outside and getting tangled in the drapery cord. René Clemente (boy-René) maintains the hypnotic stillness of an Egyptian cat statue, but with eyes frantically scanning the fascinating prey: two points of intensity capering across absolutely uncanny immobility. René Ceballos (girl-René) as a kitten in a frenzy of mouse chasing, perpetually confused by its failure to capture. I do Dharma[5] sneaking into the bathtub to

[5] Defiant pet of my Haight-Ashbury commune in the 70s.

take a vindictive dump. Cynthia Onrubia takes *her* dump in the backyard, sniffing at the turd, then directing a withering glance at a human caught watching her.

Trevor: "I must congratulate you all for committing so completely and accurately to the internalizing of the exercise. Every one of you avoided the temptation to perform or externalize, and thus to betray the intention of the inquiry." He talks about the difference between expressing a captured essence and imitating—discouraging the latter. The absence of self-consciousness, the "unawareness of being looked at" is what will create the innocence he spoke of yesterday as the key to the show.

Wednesday 11 august Day 3

Major, *major* breakthrough on this, the day devoted to group and tribal exploration. After class (a bit harder than yesterday's, but the *dancer*-dancers complained as well; apparently it's Graham-work of a type few have mastered), we did mirror exercises expressing welcome, then ecstasy (a big connection with Hector M. on this one!), then despair, which shifted back to ecstasy (tremendous exchange with Ken Page on this, Jewish and black racial memory interchanging at profound soul levels). Then back to circle, and the "telephone" exercise of passing a gesture through hand pressure around the group. Trevor observes that distortion arises from the mind's interference and evaluation, instead of the right hand reflexively duplicating what the left has felt. We get to the point of traveling around the circle five or six times without altering the impulse. Then the introduction of an emotional communication distorts the gesture again. Trevor again suggests that we leave our minds out of it and the process resumes, more effectively. Trevor has one more exercise, but we must break for lunch. Remember whom you sat between, he cautions. Since I'm between Tim & girl-René , my established buddies, we all go to a Japanese restaurant they discovered yesterday, joined by Reed Jones, the swing (who defines himself as "pure Norman Rockwell"), and Cynthia, a tough little show-biz cookie who announces that she and I will get along great—she loves my "sick humor."

Ninety minutes later we all link hands, ordered as before but standing, as Trevor announces something "really difficult." With closed eyes, we are to carefully examine the hands we are holding (smelling is also permitted). Then we are to imagine an explosion, flinging us to distant corners of the room, spinning as we go, till we are completely disoriented. Eyes still shut and in silence, we are to attempt to find our adjoining partners once more. Off we go. There is no one around me. I head toward the sound of shuffling feet. I take a hand, which feels wrong and I release it. Height is a clue, also clothing texture. At length, I feel a hand which could be René's. We sniff, explore bodies and hair, then squeeze hands affirmingly and move about together. Chains are beginning to form. I take a hand whose size is Tim's. Scent, hair, all agree. I stay put. Soon (less than five minutes all together) there is silence and calm, and Trevor bids us open our eyes. All twenty-six people have returned to their original companions and the whole circle is in its original position relative to the room. The look on every face is identical, and a wondrous whoop of joy erupts! Trevor beams. Coffee break.

Now we return to our observed cat improvs, but in the smaller studio.[6] Looking out windows, playing with window-shade strings, chasing tails. Quite immersed in catness. Only now there is free group interplay. Chasing shoes around the room, reacting as one to the sound of danger, waves of cat-people tumbling, sweeping, and skittering about the room. (Still modeled on neurotic little Dharma, I hide under chairs mostly, but watch the others with mingled fear and fascination.)

At last, Trevor calls a halt: "Your commitment and involvement leave me absolutely speechless. I felt like an imposter and an intruder."

He is full of praise and encouragement, and he announces that the next three days will concentrate on learning the opening number. "We'll be calling upon your skills, but don't lose touch with the feeling you've discovered, as we'll return to that work when next we can." The cast applauds him.

[6] Rehearsals spread among a suite of rooms at the Bennett Studios, 890 Broadway.

Sat, 14 August Day 6

As predicted, three days of routining. My inner thighs are so sore from class and crouching. But the exhilaration is tremendous. Learning snatches of combination and putting them all together. Then stopping because we can go no further till we've learned more song from Stanley, whose own singing sounds like E.T. He warns us constantly about exact breath taking and cut-offs, having earlier explained that he'll be visible only by TV monitor. "I won't be able to help you; I'll be in another room." "Playing cards," suggests Donna King, of the punk-black hair. "Possibly," he concurs.

The energy level is so high. The dancers have begun to strut their stuff. I marvel at their prowess: Tim doing sixteen grand pirouettes en l'air, Whitney topping him with twenty, Steve Gelfer, my understudy, practicing back flips, and always the amazing Ken Ard, scissoring through the air with stunning grand jetés. Herman Sebek, the beautiful Dutch-Indonesian, doing anything. During one break, after Trevor has conducted a circle-go-round of everyone saying one syllable of "Once more un-to the breach, dear friends" and trying to make it sound sensible, Terry Mann (Rum Tum Tugger to the life) sits at the piano and slams out "Take It to the Streets." Everyone begins to sing and dance and the song becomes "Take It to the Breach." We *really get down!* Trevor comes in and *kvells.*[7]

Gillie works painstakingly, polishing as she goes (her assistant Joanne is superb in this regard), and by Friday afternoon we have a big chunk of the opening. And we're selling it already! I can't believe how healthy I feel!

Saturday morning we put the button on "Jellicle Cats." It's dynamite. (I notice, amidst all the company spirit, that tigerish Debbie hasn't been around for several days. I ask girl-René, who repeats a rumor that she made a stink about her contract and left the show. "I've worked with her," she adds. "We never got along." An interesting surgical removal.) Harry Groener, a very witty man—he and Terry are the class wisecrackers—asks if now is the time for the male cats to spray the audience. "Some people can walk on a wire, me, I spray."

"I thought you'd been fixed," pipes Donna K.

I have to leave early for a costume fitting at Parsons-Meares. John Napier arrives as I do. He's such as gem, always Mr. Cool, but with a sly twinkle just below the surface. (Previous day I'd asked him to show me the Growltiger set again. "I couldn't wait for you to ask," he grinned.) The pneumatic-shoulder device has arrived.[8] John and Richard, its

---

7 Yiddish: to be gratified with enjoyment.

8 For my big 2nd-act number, in which frail Gus the Theatre Cat transforms into the bravura & comically villainous Growltiger.

creator, examine the various tubes, pipes, and tanks that tangle together in back. John wants a vacuum pump to make the shoulders lie flatter before the blow-up. "Can do," says Richard. My tunic slips on over it and we have a go. The gas, which is cold, fills the shoulders very slowly—*shvach*.[9] But when the full shape is blown up, it's hilarious. We need to reduce it to seven seconds, says John. "Can do," says Richard, but we need a bigger solenoid and an extra backup tank. Then John has a flash. What if we eliminate the expanding stomach and stuff all the mechanics into a belly pouch that's concealed beneath the Gus robe? Less gas, time, and power are required, plus I'll be free to roll on my back. We rejoice and consent. I sport around in my giant shoulders, each the size of a human head, and declaim Richard III: "But I that am not shaped for sportive tricks, nor made to court an amorous looking glass . . ." John picks up the cue "sent before my time into this breathing world."

It's 5 to 3. My whole lunch hour has been consumed. Fortunately there's some cantaloupe in the shop and I devour two luscious wedges and bid everyone good-bye, till Richard returns in two weeks with the altered pneumatic tunic. I grab a fast-food egg foo yung and gobble it up in the cab downtown.

9 Yiddish: feeble

Work in progress on the very top of "Jellicle Songs." I occupy the spot that Reed's been marking—impressed by the speed and clarity with which he teaches me what I've missed—and the number proceeds till we break to learn "The Addressing of Cats." Ken Page blows everyone away with his solo, and the chorale leaves Stanley speechless with delight. "Pre-t-ty good," he purrs.

"Well, what a week," marvels Trevor. Monday we'll return to the improvs and more character exploration, but for now it's a day off, though I'm so thrilled with the work that's underway that I'd gladly return tomorrow. Or so it seems . . .

Day Off. To Edith's.[10] Lying on Westport beach. Visualizing faces of the company. Missing them, but deeply absorbing the past week's work. Swimming feels great. Edith says I've never seemed so happy.

SECOND WEEK

Mon, 16 Aug, Day 7

Hugs and kisses at the coffee table as we regroup. Janet and I shared the same feelings of missing everyone—so did most

[10] Edith Harper, a painter-poet-therapist thirty years my senior, with a friendly house on the Connecticut shore.

others. Great class with Joanne. Gillie's off shooting the commercial with Tim and girl-René, whose absence creates a noticeable void, not just because of their spiritual contribution, but simply that the group has become tight enough to sense missing elements. A long choreographic clean-up session, very useful. Bonnie S. gets freaked out by a traffic problem and Betty in the most clear-hearted way compels her to deal with it, rather than sink into her usual reaction of impotent whining. Wouldn't it be great to get Bonnie permanently off it? This is just the company to do it, too.

Trevor takes over, brilliantly explicating "The Naming of Cats" line by line, drawing unexpected meaning from every word and image. How must he handle Shakespeare? We go around the circle reciting line by line, then in unison, then again in turn (but switching positions, as Trevor announces with superbly understated irony, "You don't want to get used to the same lines—that would make you feel secure.") A subtle and flexible group reading develops, which the introduction of piano accompaniment reduces back to singsong, which Trevor wickedly imitates till we get it better.

After lunch—and a birthday cake for Christine (eighteen today; Trevor remarks that he's never seen anyone blow out fourteen candles so fast)—we do a major improv. Warming up with an add-on machine game, we turn at last to our own characters, working from the traits so apologetically suggested last week. We walk and stretch and preen, then Trevor has us feel rain and run for shelter, then come out again to see a rainbow. Then we find the other member of the pairs that Trevor reads off—Gus going with Jellylorum. Bonnie saunters shyly up to me. I encourage her to approach without seeming to—enjoying her warmth and attention but remembering that my "star status" forbids too much intimacy. She gladly tolerates my conditions, manifesting great loyalty and devotion, and perfect willingness to humor and even support my eccentricity. All this we discuss afterwards and as per Trevor's instruction, create a vignette to exemplify our discoveries. He then directs each pair to another pair. We perform for Grizabella (Betty) and Victoria (Cynthia), then they for us, and we discuss. They react very favorably and perceptively to our piece. Likewise we admire the clarity of the action of innocent Vic approaching Griz as a playmate, unaware of her pariah status, and Griz's confusion and mixed panic and pleasure at being so approached. Then we create a scene for the four of us: Vic approaching the shivering Gus, he recoiling, Jelly showing Vic the proper mode of approach, warming me as before, I growing vain and flirtatious, then Jelly putting her foot down on games between Vic and Griz.

Then we join two other foursomes, first as audiences. Tim and René do an electric mating dance, he using the mirror-imaged Janet and boy-René to persuade girl-René that he just wants to play. Initially hostile, she is won over by his high jinks. René and Janet are mystically attuned to the last move—spellbinding—and Tim is dazzling as he springs twice to the vertical from all fours. Then Ken Ard and Wendy Edmead do their S & M thing, intersected by the more boisterous and sleazy Hector and Donna till the two men confront in a stunning macho duel—Hector feeling he is almost a match for the malevolent Macavity, but ultimately not daring to strike. Intense violent energy—intensely theatrical. I feel that our group is nowhere near this level, but as we proceed the response is tremendous—laughter and tears coming swiftly together. Everyone seems deeply moved.

We form a circle of twelve and discuss what we received, what we attempted. The talk is excited, overlapping, agitated, when Trevor reluctantly interrupts to say it's 6:30 and we must stop. We all want to stay and finish, but it must be postponed. A fantastic afternoon, rich in promise.

Thurs, 19 aug Day 10

So now we're deep into routining. Classes with Gillie or Joanne every morning, dance work till lunch, then afternoons of singing with Stanley. The whole opening number is now finished and it is a gas. But we've also had two reminders of the fragile state of grace in which we function. Tuesday at a run-through of the very top of the number, Janet stubbed her toe during her twin rollout with René. She limped off the floor and at first no one knew what had happened or how severe the injury was. You could feel everyone shudder. Then yesterday, doing his fourth or fifth back flip for the Ball Invitation, Steve Gelfer was thrown by a slower tempo and fell on his hand. Just re-visioning it makes me flinch. It looked like he might have broken his arm, but he was just a little stunned and bruised his palm and hip. All the same, both events gave quite a shake to the ensemble's sense of giddy joy—we forget in our joy what risks we are taking.

The musical work is marvelous. Bonnie S. and I were pulled out of the Ball number for long enough to work on "Gus" with Stanley. It's a beautiful number, far more than the London album suggested to me. A wonderful simplicity in the steadily unwinding, subtly varying melody line as Gus breaks out of his shell and recalls his past, on and on and on. Bonnie's line is lovely, too, and she sang it with great beauty and tenderness, though constantly belittling and faulting her own efforts (not a trait to which I am prone). If she could forgive herself as wholeheartedly as her character forgives and humors Gus, she'd enjoy the process more and we all would. Hopefully I can assist in this area. Trevor came in and listened some, then commented that I could sing the music with less rhythmic fidelity, finding more conversational patterns of delivery. As Stanley says, Gus is just a simple, honest cat, and here is just talking, *talking* unpretentiously about things he once did.

Some wonderful choral numbers—"Skimbleshanks" with its hurtling 13/8 meters and headlong harmonies—and

Willie Rosario's going to be marvelous in it. He's a marvelous dancer and a hilarious comic—his moment of peering out from under Ken Page's arm is a scream. The haunting beauty of "Old Deuteronomy" and the insolent pizzazz of "Rum Tum Tugger," which suits Terry Mann perfectly. And the rewritten "Journey to the Heaviside Layer" will be nothing short of sublime, with its invocation of earlier musical phrases.

Trevor has remained mainly on the sidelines for the past few days, watching and conferring, occasionally stepping out to clarify a moment. But the fact is that his mere presence establishes a center of calm and inspiration that affects everybody. When he appeared the other day in white linen trousers with pink shirt and sport jacket instead of his usual blue nondescripts (en route to lunch with Raquel Welch), everyone ogled and hooted and he took it like the marvelous good sport he is. Yesterday, having worn my hairpiece for the rehearsal photographers, I asked him when he first realized I'd worn it at my auditions, reminding him of the irony of his commending my "innocence" at the time. "When the fact is I'm a cheap liar," he finished my thought. I adore him.

After rehearsal yesterday we were invited to a party at Century Café to honor the start of rehearsals—no press. Cameron Mackintosh came over to say he'd heard that my dance classes had made me one of the most agile members of the cast. I was thrilled—even if there was a scent of hyperbole. Just as long as I don't look like a ringer. Also a great moment with Trevor, when he asked if I knew who Judi

Dench was. "She doubled as your Hermione and Perdita,"[11] I said, and he turned half around with amazement. "I've been a fan of yours since *The Relapse*," I continued, and he doubled over to think of something so far back. We talked some about that production and experienced a great deepening of our bond.

Today Andrew brought in the aria—or at least the tune (having misplaced the Italian translation of Eliot), which is fabulous ersatz Puccini. We set the key best suited to me and concertina (E flat modulating to F) and I sang it a couple of times in gibberish Italian, at which Stanley marveled. The exact finish isn't set yet, but it'll climax on a high A—what a treat!

Cabbed uptown after work with Tim and Joanne, who was upset because Gillie had snapped at her during a dance rehearsal. Tim noted the stress Gillie's under to get everything staged and urged Joanne not to take it personal. Later I called him to meet for dinner (my shiatsu having been canceled), and we had a great time talking about the show, life, God, and dancing. He also mentioned the fact of his year-old relationship with a man in California named Matt. (Lucky Matt!) Having thus uprooted, in his typically gracious way, any romantic expectation I might be cultivating, he invited me over to his apartment, a small but cozy one-bedroom in an elegant brownstone with a balcony and view of the river,

11 *The Winter's Tale*, Royal Shakespeare Company 1969, when I was a student at LAMDA.

and played the "Rumpleteazer" tape (over which lyric he keeps tripping). I sang him the aria, which he loved—especially the falsetto B-flat meow, which I just thought of—and then we listened to a tape of his guru, Terry Cole Whittaker, who had some stirring things to say, especially about God being her source, not the world or anything in it. I left when an expected friend of Tim's showed up, and he gave me a brotherly parting kiss. What an amazing sweet man! And once again life offers a mix of disappointment with blissful love. May the latter prevail.

Sat., 21 Aug Day 12

Yesterday I was pulled out of dance rehearsal—just at the point where the Ball becomes too hard for me to do anyway, to work with Stanley on learning "Bustopher Jones."[12] Then Trevor and Andrew came in with the aria lyric. We explored different modes of placing words and accents, of which there are too many to really fit the tune, and finally came up with a solution. I kept trying to get Andrew to listen to my B-flat interpolation, but he kept holding forth in his inexorable way, until Trevor got what I was up to and opened a gap. I meow-sang for them and they loved it, Andrew agreeing to use it. Trevor gave me a bear hug, then took me aside to talk

[12] Rehearsals had begun with no one assigned to the role of the pompous snob Bustopher, which in London had been doubled by the actor playing Old Deuteronomy.

21

about Bustopher. They wanted to hear me do it, but were concerned about its possibly undermining Gus. I expressed the same ambivalence. He put his arm around me and said, "I love you and I think you're wonderful, and I don't want to start you out with an experience of rejection." I assured him that either decision would be fine with me, because I'd gladly do Bustopher, and I'd happily concentrate on Gus alone. So I'll work on it and show them next week.

The rehearsal process is fragmenting as dancers work in one room, singers in another, and others hang around for a call in the greenroom. It's unavoidable but I feel a lowering of energy—mixed with downright exhaustion after a long dance rehearsal—that's a distinct shift from earlier days. And some dissatisfaction with Gillie's choreography is buzzing about.

This morning I worked on Bustopher with the three ladies and also on Gus—which I'd had some breakthroughs with at home last night. Stanley liked them both (when he says, "That's good, Steve," in his uninflected way, it means there's no criticism), but he suggested that Gus might be simpler. Then the ensemble came to learn their part. I sat up front and soloed for the first time. What a treat. The choral sound is fabulous; everyone should have a chance to step out and hear it. Cynthia and Janet gave me special winks of approval.

Gillie was working the Ball with just a quartet of men, and the rest of us sat in the hallway memorizing and practicing music (Stanley wants us off book by Wednesday). Again a wonderful group feeling. Then Stanley called me in to do the aria, "Bustopher," and "Gus" for Andrew, who liked all three. Regarding "Bustopher," he said to Stanley, "I don't see any problem with similarity." Stanley replied, "Yes, but I can understand his point," as if I ought not to be privy to this exchange. Draw the veil. Andrew wanted more singing and less speaking on "Gus" (not surprising), but they both agreed that it was ready for Trevor to work on it. Bonnie came in to hear the aria and we hit a wonderful unison high A. It will be thrilling.

Lunch with Timmy, he very distressed. He senses major problems with Gillie's choreography—namely that she designs at reduced speed and then expects everyone to perform too many steps at high tempo. Too much effort for too little payoff. The result will be messy and the critics will howl. And he's frustrated by the Mistoffelees solo, too airy-fairy, balletic, and cute. "I'm already cute, I don't need to dance it." He apologized for whining and bitching, but he was obviously truly disturbed, not knowing how to approach Gillie to adapt her work more to his style. "I'm a fabulous jazz dancer, I'm hot and sexy, but I'm not Wayne Sleep."[13] He wants to improvise for Gillie just to show her his style and his character ideas, and what stops him is lack of confidence. Which I sought to build up, offering him the loft to practice in beforehand. I also pointed out his obligation to distinguish between the gripe of Tim the dancer who must do eight shows a week, and Tim the frustrated choreographer.

[13] Star of the Royal Ballet, who created the role in London.

"I don't begin to have the ideas she has," he admitted, "but I know how to dance close to the ground. All her stuff is ballet, up in the air, but cats are down. She doesn't choreograph for the ground." In his gentle and low-key way he was really upset. I can see how much he expects from the Mistoffelees role, and how frustrated he is that it might go the wrong way. "Michael Bennett told me I was his best dancer," he confided, and it didn't surprise me. He really is sensational (and others, who presumably aren't in love with him, agree). I reiterated my offer of rehearsal space and urged him to think it over, and not be afraid of being thought a troublemaker.

After lunch we did improvs with Trevor, the first extended work session with him in quite some time—since Monday's curtailed one. At first the attempt to recapture the foursome improvs was either technical & heartless, or felt & under-energized. But eventually we got into the swing, doing a long twelve-person exercise of coming into a new space and having to shelter from the rain in any of three possible refuges. Some very good, spontaneous, inter-feline discoveries.

Then our group looked at the group of eight and vice versa. Night and day. They projected a clear sense of clan—hierarchical, intergenerational, and unified. Harry was especially brilliant as Munkustrap going out to meet a perceived danger. Simple, honest, and utterly direct. Willie was hilarious, also Terry and the kittens—Christina and Whitney. By contrast our group was, as Terry said, "Peyton Place."

Then Trevor: "As we all know, there are just two kinds of improvisations. (There's a contentious statement and I always begin contentious statements with 'As we all know.')" He proceeded to explain the Stanislavskian vs. Brechtian modes, and he proposed a scenario for our first attempt at the latter: cats playing, Grizabella to enter and be rejected, Macavity to enter and attempt to kidnap Demeter, Deuteronomy to enter and repel him, and the rest to express their gratitude to Old D. Although everyone is tired from a strenuous week, some powerful things happen in these final afternoon hours. The response to Griz, the absolute impersonal sense that her presence violates some essential taboo is more terrifying than any personal animosity could be. The willingness of the group—*as group*—to stand up to Macavity, though not what Trevor intended, is thrilling and the devotion to Old D. creates a great mood of awe and unity. And on that note we break, in anticipation of the transition to two legs and upright stance.

THIRD WEEK

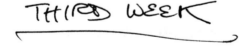

Monday 23 August Day 13

The day's first big news came as eyewitness reports from Janet Hubert and Diane Fratantoni (and later Trevor) that lines went around the block at the Winter Garden on this first morning of box office sales. Yippee!

Rest of the morning I worked with Stanley on "Bustopher," "Gus," and the aria. Trevor came in and watched Bonnie and me do "Gus," which he liked a great deal. He talked in some depth about the character relations, about using the text to establish Jellylorum's concern and respect for Gus. What he missed was the sense of how truly important "Firefrorefiddle"[14] was—how it was the one thing Gus did that really worked, his moment of true glory and pride. He promised to work with us line by line, but for the moment called the work wonderful.

Bonnie and I went up to the Winter Garden at lunch. Police barricades left on the sidewalk for the crowd that had accumulated before the torrential afternoon rain came. Inside, a furor of construction. The WG almost unrecognizable with our apron jutting way past the proscenium, and the ceiling covered over with the already magical starry-sky panels. Bonnie's inquiry about my street-singing past prompted a thumbnail autobiography. She was fascinated by my Haight-Ashbury saga. She's really coming out and I'm sure will prove a marvelous scene partner.

She went back downtown, but I hung around, not due back till 4:30. I sat in Wolf's Deli and suddenly started to

14 Gus the Theatre Cat is an old derelict who claims to have been a star in his youth, perpetually recalling "that moment of mystery when I made history as Firefrorefiddle the Fiend of the Fell."

bliss out, as I experienced myself as a simple sojourner on this planet, working/playing my way back to God. All this great enterprise-creativity-opportunity is part of the path of return—raising the sparks, in the Hasidic mode.[15]

Back at the studio, we learned the first part of "Growltiger." Trevor did a great riff on melodrama for the benefit of everyone doing the narration: how to justify the necessary overstatement and extremeness. I was so inspired that when we ran through and I got to my line "the Terror of the Thames," I threw my chair against the wall. Some people jumped; Trevor and John Napier smiled amazedly, and I felt rather embarrassed. But it was a statement.

At 6:30, Trevor and Gillian and Joanne came in to audition "Bustopher." First Trevor said, "Now after you do it a couple of times, I won't say anything. There's a lot of conferring to do, so don't be disappointed."

"Will you say anything between the times?" I asked.

He said, "Yes, perhaps." I dove in. I could see they all liked it. Trevor then directed it differently, asking me to be more solid and self-satisfied, selling the number less and simply receiving the expected adulation. I did it all again and had some good new flashes. Trevor said, "Well, your invention and skill are, as always, wonderful—" ("Such invention!" Gillie concurred)—"and I assure you they will not be the

[15] Hasidism's understanding of the life process is founded on the idea that every created form contains a spark of Divine Life & the soulful person's task is to raise those sparks lovingly into conscious union with their source.

topic of our discussion. And I promise I won't wreck any more of your weekends." They thanked me profusely and I went home. Their thoughtfulness is utterly astounding!

Tuesday 24 August Day 14

Great long warm-up class with Gillie, then a review of the opening, which went rather well, considering how long it's been ("Very nearly very good," as Gillie says). Then I watched as much of the Ball as had been put together in the last few days while I've been elsewhere. Incredible. It begins with a wonderful balletic solo for Tim, culminating in a high cabriole as he encounters Hector. Add Willie and Ken Ard and a fabulous, strong male quartet ensues. Enter Donna King in an electrifying slinky solo, which girl-René makes a duet, then quartet with Wendy and Janet. Four new men. Then a gorgeous balletic duo of Tim and Herman, superbly matched. Then everybody. Wow, wow, and double-wow!

Lunch with Tim. He's feeling much better about the work (everyone seems to—maybe it was the day off), also getting secure in singing "Mungojerrie." We talked about press agents, about why we want to become known (and what for), he shared his insecurity about a club act (singing, facing an audience) and his high hopes for the show. Our usual wonderful exchange.

Work on the duet with Bonnie. Her soprano register is great and our unison high A is sensational. She laughs at all my invention and is loosening up more and more. And yet, while we do this work I feel regretfully absent from the rest of the company at the Ball. Not that I could keep up, but simply that I'm not with them, in there working as a group. So it's a relief when everyone comes in to sing for the last two hours. Stanley teaches us "Grizabella the Glamour Cat" (we also have our first brief moment singing a snatch of "Memory"—sooo gorgeous). Trevor does another brilliant exposition of text (Tottenham Court Road=a place of desolation—not even the "teeming late-night malpractice" of Soho) and then Betty sings—her first solo before the group—and it's goosebump time! Great sound, great acting, great feeling—another star pops out. Every time she was totally different, but always equally arresting and fine. God, this show is blessed.

I told Trevor that Bonnie and I were thinking of visiting the old actor's home. "Better be careful, Steve, they'll keep you there," he said.

Wed 26 August Day 15

This morning more work on the Ball. The run-through was even better than yesterday's. How I wish I had the physical control of a real dancer. I feel privileged to be in this company, as I promptly proceeded to tell everyone. (They all replied that it was mutual, though what I've done to impress anyone as yet escapes me.)

What a range of styles: quirky Willie, virile Hector, slinky Donna, regal Janet, girl-René so angular, Timmy so elegant, Cynthia so passionate, electrifying Kenneth. Then Gillie called everyone together and made a speech. "Darlings, please forgive me but I'm going to say something harsh. I know how painful the work is, I've danced it all through myself with Joanne. I know how it tears at your guts and your legs and your backs. But, though I won't mention names, I saw a couple of people marking here and there, and I must insist that you do it full out from here on in. If you don't get over the pain threshold now, you'll never do it by opening night. You must go through it now and keep on until it's so natural that it doesn't hurt anymore. It's the only way you'll find the stamina and endurance to make it work, and the only way you can get the images to become real. Do you all agree?" She was at her best, and we all applauded.

Then Bonnie and I had a long work session with Trevor, first on the aria, then on "Gus." He talked about absurd romanticism, about the actor-manager tradition leading directly to Fairbanks, then to Flynn and Lancaster, about the nineteenth century theater's curious mix of exact physical naturalism with inflated overacting, about traces of Jellylorum's propriety surfacing through Griddlebone's "Stop-it-I-like-it" flirtation. Before we sang Bonnie said apologetically that she had scarcely warmed up . . . he cut straight through and said, "But are you having fun, Bonnie?" to which she unhesitatingly replied, "Yes." And we sang the shit out of it (me atop the piano at first), continually breaking each other up, to his unconcealed delight.

As for "Gus," it was the greatest ninety minutes I've ever spent in rehearsal. He analyzed text ("seventy speeches seems like a lot to anyone who doesn't know that an actor learns 3000 in a season"), relationships (Jellylorum's describing Gus' frailties as if he weren't there, but recognizing some things as truly sensitive matters, e.g., the palsy), excised my nodded bow to the gallery ("Too early on to go into your fantasy world—what would you mime if I said you'd played a championship season of baseball? Just the pleasure of having it be true."), and even suggested blocking, but always motivationally. His expression is so lucid and his direction so easy to follow that with each run-through he'd say "Smashing" and add the next level. He said something about tearing one's *kishkas*[16] out and gave me the same look he did last week when using another Yiddish phrase, as if it were in quotes and he expected me to be surprised at his use of it. A delightful moment, one of many from this courtly, affectionate, brilliant, profound, and altogether mind-blowing man.

16 yiddish: guts

Thursday 26 August   Day 16

Gillie suspended class this morning (Cynthia offered barre at
9:30 in her inimitable goofy dragon-lady style) to press
through to the finish of the Ball. She worked all morning (I
sat around idling and worked on the aria and "Gus" around
noon with Stan and Bonnie) and by 1:15 was only two meas-
ures from the end. She stopped and ran it from the top,
starting with the "Jellicle Cats" poem. I stepped out at my
usual moment and crossed down to watch from the front.

The familiar section was better than when I'd last
looked; then all the new stuff started. I'd seen snatches of it
but had no sense of its continuity. As it built and built, you
could begin to see everybody's strain and pain and agony.
Groans and moans began to break forth. The non-dancers,
starting with Betty B., began to cheer everyone on: "Come
on, Donna! Go for it! Yeah, yeah!" Rooting and urging like at
a sports event and somehow, in spite of the slips and blurs
and glazed expressions, they kept on. René Ceballos, always
so willing and energized, seemed about to faint. There was
no sparkle or flair, just sheer grit, and with everyone offstage clapping out the rhythm and cheering, they got to the
finish. Everyone burst into applause and kept up a sustained
ovation. Timmy collapsed on the floor, people fell into one
another's arms. It was stunning.

In the locker room en route to lunch, everyone was

abuzz with comprehension of the challenge posed by getting it right and doing it eight times a week. "We've got to run this once every day from now on," said Harry, to unanimous agreement. People were dazed, breathless, exhilarated. We who had watched it were agog, knowing that surely every audience would have the same response: pouring out their hearts to encourage and assist the phenomenal feat of endurance before them. What a curtain!

Lunch with Trevor at Brownie's (I didn't realize he dined with the company). He told great stories about his official visit to Russia (the government censor rejecting a production of *Twelfth Night* because the line "Thou art as dark as the Egyptians in their fog," was a threat to international relations; the *Don Juan* where Sganarelle stomped to the back of the house and Don J. delivered his hypocrisy harangue to the whole auditorium, which rose and cheered as at a musical number), about Peter Brook, and we talked about *The Winter's Tale* ("Oh, she's warm" being his favorite line in the Shakespearean canon). Then Herman and I sunned in the park till our 4 P.M. call, talking about star quality, about love and joy as the real factors of self-expression, etc. He has the most beautiful innocence and desire to learn and grow—really perfect typecasting as a kitten. When we got back everyone was assembled in rank and file, holding giant knives and forks and learning the Gumbie Cat tap routine. A new number! The show goes on.

Friday 27 August Day 17

Not called till 3, I baked a Swedish Tea Ring that was instantly devoured. Stanley called me in to learn a change in the aria, then showed me the "Bustopher" cut. "You mean I'm doing it? Is this official?" Well, sort of, he said, and said we'd ask Trevor, who he had assumed had already told me. So after Gillie put me into my spot at the opening of "Tugger" (the day's project), Trevor took me into his official dressing room (the sanctum—I felt honored—and how understatedly elegant and plush) to discuss how to play Bustopher. The problem being that I'd have already begun to establish Gus and would require a major facial disguise, and that no inkling of the power of my voice must come yet to undercut the aria's shock value. He wants a Brit caricature, that dramatically sets up the arrival of Mistoffelees to entertain the guest of honor with "Mungojerrie." The accent laid on with a trowel. A charm number—à la Mostel in soft shoe—fat man above, nimble feet below. I need to twinkle, but not overwhelm. It will be a challenge, as my apprehension is that we not try to sneak the number past people—so I have to create a full performing persona that offers no hint of the things to come in Act Two.

Anyway, what a relief to work on "Tugger." It feels like we're in a show again, routining a numbah-number. Terry is marvelous—a male Mae West, exuding sensuality while spoofing it. The little character vignettes that pepper the number are delightful: clever, witty, unpretentious musical comedy staging at its best. The company seems happy to be doing something so playful after all the strain of the Ball.

Sat 28th August Day 18

How did this week fly by so fast? Hard to believe it's already Saturday and we play our first preview in under four weeks. Work on the Ball all morning. The big event was when Trevor caught sight of me writing in this journal, yanked it out of my hand and refused to return it, with an indignant "What's this? A journal?" "Have you ever had a Boswell before?" I asked. "Indeed I have, and it was one of the worst experiences of my life." He proceeded to tell his account of being ripped off by the *Nicholas Nickleby* book during which I pried this notebook out of his hands, with assurances that publication was not my intent.[17] Never seen him so vehement and worked up—a whole new TN!

Lunch in Madison Park with Tim and Herman. A gorgeous sunny day and we all took off our shirts. Sitting between the two most beautiful men in the company—my gaze just ambled from one to the other, browsing ecstatically.

17 after 19 years, I invoke the statute of limitations!

A musical rehearsal-review with Stan all afternoon. During the Growltiger section Bonnie and I finally sprung the aria and duet on the company. I don't know when I've ever been so nervous, unveiling my specialty before this group I've grown so to admire and respect. I even used my music sheets, which I've done without for days, just to have a hand prop and someplace to look! But it went over like crazy, several times interrupted by laughter, gasps, whoops, and applause, and got a prolonged and thunderous ovation at the finish, of the kind the Ball received on its first run-through. "Boy, was that worth waiting for," said Bob Hoshour. Bonnie and I were so thrilled and relieved—it's bound to stop the show at this rate. Timmy said, "It was so beautiful and *passionate*, I almost cried, even while I was still laughing."

Stan broke the men early and Tim and I went into the small studio. I showed him the mime I've been working on for my walk off the plank. He thought it was very funny, clear, and precise, and he urged me to show it to Trevor without fail. Then we talked about his approach to "Mungojerrie," and I showed him the LAMDA "P-r-r-m-m" exercise, which immediately increased his resonance. Then I vocalized him through some scales and breath octaves, and he began to produce a bright and very focused sound *in alt*, going all the way up to a beautifully supported B flat, which he'd never sung before. He was thrilled, to say the least, and warm in his praise for how proximity to me was building his vocal confidence a lot. Boy, have we got a great thing going!

Fourth Week

Tues 31 Aug Day 20

Raced in yesterday morning from Connecticut on a train forty-five minutes late, only to discover that I wasn't needed till 3. So I spoke to David Taylor (our Stage Manager) about the dressing room issue. He said it was tight, but he was sympathetic to my wanting my own space to prepare for the aria, and he agreed that it would be perfectly appropriate for me to ask Tyler,[18] with whose decision he would go along. So I went straight to the office, where I learned Tyler had left for the theater. Not to be deterred, I followed after, preparing my arguments, counter-defenses, etc. Met Tyler at the joint-jumping Winter Garden, and he took me to lunch to talk in private. As soon as I asked for my own room, he concurred, no argument was even necessary, and he said he'd call David that afternoon to set it up. What a mindblower! Then he pumped me for info about the show and explained his philosophy of fair-dealing management ("Life is too short"). We walked back to the theater where, at John Napier's invitation I walked on the sloping boat deck floor.

[18] Tyler Gatchell, the general manager & boss of all things contractual.

37

An extremely steep rake—rather alarming—but at the top, where the aria starts, I'm at balcony eye-level, in full command of the house. Oh God, I can't wait! A great deal of the set is up and the Disneyland effect is already strong.

The afternoon brought music rehearsal with Stanley and more of the same this morning. We did the aria again, this time with Trevor present, and got another hand. Spent the rest of the morning staging "Pekes and Pollicles," a number I find utterly delightful, especially as done by Harry G., a totally enchanting, witty, and authoritative performer. Baby Christine is wonderful in it, as a Pekinese squaring off at boy-René, who's hilarious. After lunch, we ran the opening through "Gumbie" (needs work, especially the tap) and "Tugger," then the Ball—it's getting easier for everyone but also kinda sloppy today. Timmy, suffering from an intestinal virus, marked a lot, as did others. Then the rest of the day was back to "Pekes and Pollicles." Gillie worked out a tremendous routine for Ken Ard's Rumpus Cat. While they were working, Janet H. came over to me and girl-René and said, "I can't watch this. He's doing it all wrong technically and it scares the shit out of me." It never entered my mind. René said lots of dancers—Nureyev—throw themselves around that way, it's not as dangerous as it looks—especially for an acrobat. But it was amazing to see how deep Janet's upset was.

Thurs 2 Sept   Day 22

Not called till 3 yesterday—brought a poppy seed cake, which made a big hit. Watched the routining of "Skimbleshanks," a very inventive number and Willie utterly delightful. Precise, quick and if possible even more charming with his horn-rim glasses (having had trouble with his contacts). He will make a tremendous hit. Sang a bit afterwards, but basically an uninspiring day.

Company meeting this morning. David warned us of the tight spacing backstage at the Winter Garden and advised us to be prepared to cope with the pressures when we move uptown—gotta stay disciplined. Then we arrived at a company intention to ask for a switch to Tuesday-Sunday playing schedule (after February) and a more equitable house seat policy than five pairs *in toto* per night.

After a really good warm-up, we ran the Ball again. Sloppy, but definitely an improvement in stamina. Gillie gave wonderful notes afterwards. ("Too pretty, Cynthia, it's not 'Look at *me*, I'm a ballereeena,'"). She's every bit as clear and exact and subtle as Trevor, and despite the pressure of time (as David said, "We're not exactly behind, but it would be nice if we were further along."), her humor is very much intact. ("What's the image on the reach?" I asked. "Just ecstasy, darling." Or: "That was horribly human, darlings.")

We went into Studio 2 to work on "The Naming of Cats" with Stanley. But we got totally bogged down in the question of how to approach rehearsing it. Do we try to set an exact musical rhythm for the unison speaking, or do we have it grow out of the acting approach? And what *is* the acting approach? Everybody had an opinion and I began to understand why it took so long to set the protocols for the Vietnam peace talks. At last, Stan, at a loss as to Trevor's intention for the number, said, "Well, how did he tell you to do it?" At that moment the door opened and TN himself walked in. Everyone burst into cheers and applause. Superb timing.

He talked about the number at great length—to him it's the biggest risk in the show for each of us, as we must work our own sections of the audience personally,[19] but without losing the unison vocal connection. We must grip the audience so totally, simultaneously affronting and engaging them, that by the time we return to the stage, they feel that this is not like any other show they've ever seen. When we're out there, they have to feel too intimidated to shift, cough, cross legs, etc. So they have to understand every last word. It's an enormous challenge, and the rehearsal didn't really help much to resolve the question of balancing personal commitment with unison diction.

After lunch, more singing with Stanley. I'm beginning to have some vocal fun and Timmy was very encouraging. Then we worked on "Growltiger" and included the aria, Andrew hear-

19 During this segment the cast moves out into the house.

ing it for the first time (evidently he grinned all the way through it). Bonnie and I played from the back of the room, and with the increase in space I tended to become correspondingly broad. It got new laughs, but I had some breath problems and some of the bel canto was lost. I'll have to work on just the right balance. But I did hit the B-flat full-out and drew some gasps. Hope I can do eight a week.

Waiting in the hallway to work on Gus with Trevor, I heard snatches of Betty's "Memory." It was hair-raising, powerfully felt, and intelligently projected. And such chops! Gradually everyone trickled out of the room and moments later I heard Betty's wild sobs, keeping up for quite some time—a major emotional release. Then she came out, embarrassed to see me, and vanished. Then everyone returned and she sang it superbly.

Trevor's focus on Gus this time was getting rid of such specifically human gestures as holding up a raised index finger and making him more catlike—yet not losing the rich sense of observed detail that has developed. After a second run, when the final "Firefrorefiddle" really choked me up, he cautioned against "manufacturing" an emotion and even though I'd felt it sincerely, I knew what he meant—producing the emotion for the audience instead of eliciting it from them. He patted and rubbed me on the heart a lot. We're into a very subtle area now. The basic work is there, the interplay with Bonnie, the inner life, and now it's time to make some specific technical choices ("cattier" gestures, less contrived old man's voice—"An actor with a voice as marvelous as yours doesn't need to confine himself to that,"—more fidelity to the musical line) and yet keep growing and investigating. I hope we do it for the company soon. I'd like some more response.

Fri 3 Sept Day 23
(FULL MOON)

Not called till 3. Spent morning preparing dinner for Timmy, Betty, and others coming over after rehearsal en route to Justin Ross' full moon meditation. Ball, "Skimbleshanks," routine routining, music rehearsal (very good work on the opening and closing, Stanley was quite happy with the accuracy). Timmy still sick—diarrhea, weakness, no appetite. It's been nearly a week now and he's looking worried and peaked. He left early to confer with a holistic healer.

Betty, Whitney, and Christine hopped in a cab with me and we went down to TriBeCa. They had the customary first-timers' blown-away reaction to the loft. I made piña coladas and we sat down to schmooze over cheese and crackers, awaiting Tim's post-appointment call. We swapped audition stories and the ladies prevailed upon me to read the opening entries of this journal. Pleasant reminders abounded for us all. Finally, I set to work preparing the meal and Tim called just as I was finishing the fish sauce. He got directions and arrived just as we were sitting to table. His diet restricted, he gazed with longing at the bottle of Grgich Hills Riesling and finally dared to sniff at its mouth. We held hands and I invoked the Sabbath queen[20] and we shared a wonderful feast of bluefish, asparagus, and millet with veggies. Such a joy to see lovely faces from the new family in my home space. Christine, at eighteen, was a bit overwhelmed, but she soaked in a lot. Before the fruit salad, I gave Tim the tour and fetched out *The Mystic in the Theatre*[21] for him to borrow. Betty began reading passages from it (particularly regaled by Duse's custom of playing no more than four or five times a week, she did a hilarious mock appeal to Bernie Jacobs to allow us the same policy), and we passed it around the table, reading pertinent sections of great insight. Communal dish-washing and off we went to the meditation, where we found both Renés, Herman, and Brian Bullard. The repetitions of the Great Invocation got us all off and the moon glowed bright and round above us and the glittering city.

[20] The inauguration of the Jewish Sabbath on Friday nights is traditionally viewed as the welcoming home of a queen, the feminine archetype of wholeness & submission to the sacred.

[21] Eva Le Gallienne's reminiscence of Eleanora Duse.

Sat 4 Sept Day 24

After warm-up, Trevor announced that we would attempt to "achieve" (a favorite word of his) a run-through of the whole show from the point of view of storyline, filling in the moments between numbers with continuity of event and character, answering everyone's questions on logistics and flow. A major order, and what with blocking everyone's moves into the house for "The Naming of Cats," return for the Invitation and so forth, we only reached the beginning of "Tugger" by lunchtime. A large party—girl-René, Bonnie, Harry, Herman, Terry, Whitney, Christine, Hector, and Donna—went in search of Italian food, leaping and skipping down the street in high abandon, despite finding the first two restaurants closed. We settled on Chinese and dined in exuberant spirits. Whitney and Herman competed in *grand jetés* on the way back, bounding off the sidewalk like young gods.

Back to the same work. Even while essentially directing traffic, it's amazing how many pains Trevor takes to motivate, clarify, and fill in. I sidled up to John Napier and said, "We're supposed to get through the whole show today," and he replied, "You've got to get used to the fact that Trevor isn't fazed by time. He'll take as long as he needs to get something right, rather than rush it through half-done."

And indeed he does. A long time working on the first Grizabella entrance, until it crackles with tension and grief. I began to understand more of TN's method. He has spent the previous weeks reiterating the facts of everyone's relationship to Grizabella, so that now, when we are essentially improvising on our feet, there is a wealth of history to draw upon, and it comes leaping forth. Betty is just electrifying. And what follows this but the silly old fart Bustopher Jones—me. Trevor leads me around the edge of the stage, sketching in the basic points of action. I punch out the bottom of a styrofoam coffee cup to make a monocle and strut around with a spoon swagger stick left over from "Gumbie." Total winging—but everyone seems to like it. I suppose it's a mark of Trevor's trust in me that he leaves me entirely to my own devices, though we haven't ever discussed the role since the day he confirmed my playing it. I'm certainly not above making a fool of myself—and do so!

The afternoon is waning, but we press on through "Mungojerrie," the first Macavity scare, the quasi-religious entrance of Old Deuteronomy (truly a magnificent moment), "Pekes and Pollicles," the Jellicle Ball, and the entrance of (and retreat from) Grizabella that closes the act. It's 6:32. Trevor says, "Well, I hope everyone's sense of the story is much clearer than when we started. I'm going back to London for two days to handle an urgent crisis at the RSC, and on Wednesday, we'll work the same way on Act Two." Enthusiastic applause.

FIFTH WK

Monday 6 Spt (LABOR DAY)

Flew in this morning from Fire Island Pines after making a
great impression at the SAGE benefit and being warmly
admired and well-wished by Chita Rivera, Patrice Munsel,
Jerry Herman, Peggy Cass, Liliane Montevecchi, Karen Akers,
et al. Really a thrill. Half an hour late for costume fitting,
however, and dead on my feet. But the Growltiger shoulders
now inflate in three seconds and the effect is sensational.
The whole costume looks great. So do the Siamese that go
with it, especially the amazing face masks.

At 3 we warmed up with the opening and went on to the
Ball. Midway through the first men's quartet, landing from a
double *tour*, Willie let out a yelp that grew into agonizing
howls, groans, and sobs. Some people helped him over to the
side, put an ice pack on his knee (an old injury) and waited.
His pain filled the room, sobs of more than physical grief—
clearly the apprehension of being unable to do the role. We
huddled or knelt together in small groups, praying, crying,
whispering, while the stage management bustled about for a
medic. Reed (his standby) massaged Willie's heart, Cynthia
held his hand, Bonnie pressed the ice to his knee, and Terry
held a compress to his forehead. Gillie came over and kissed
him. "Willie, darling, you tell the doctors to do whatever

they like as long as I can have you on opening night. It doesn't matter if you miss a few previews, you can learn a lot from sitting out here and watching, but what counts is that I have you on the 7th." Gerry Schoenfeld[22] called the head orthopedist at Bellevue and arranged for an ambulance to take Willie direct to an examination. Cynthia and Hector spoke to him in Spanish, getting his locker key and retrieving his stuff, and at last, David Taylor and Hector carried him from the room. God, how sad! Lovely, affable, funny, dances-like-popcorn Willie. We all pray for his speedy healing and return to our midst.

Rehearsal continued—the Ball from where we'd left off. Everyone marking, being extra-careful and as a result, sloppy. How fragile we are; lucky mud, as Zalman[23] says. Gillie polished what TN did on Saturday: the Macavity scare, Deut's entrance. Word came that Willie hadn't broken any-thing—a sprain and perhaps a torn ligament. The NY Yankees' orthopedist will see him tomorrow. The last half hour was a beat-to-beat staging of "Bustopher," then Gillie and I worked on it after hours. It's going to be fine, a simple little charm number, with me mincing about in my absurd fat-penguin profile. Gillie likes me eating the carnation, too, so for now it's in.

22 Chairman of the Shubert Organization
23 Zalman Schachter-Schelomi, friend & spiritual mentor.

Thurs 9 Sept Day 28

Tuesday more routining. Ran Bustopher again and it's working fine. There were camera crews from 20/20 and CBS News
watching in preparation for a Wednesday morning shoot.
Next day cameras came and they filmed the warm-up and
several numbers: Tugger, Macavity, and Grizabella. Trevor
arrived looking like he'd had too much airline food. Long
work on "Gumbie." Feeling totally bored and unused, though
I had a brief talk with TN about the Growltiger fight—he
showed me the scenario, which is very funny and inventive.
Can't wait to stage it. Showed it to Timmy at lunch by way
of assuring him how deeply Trevor cares about showing his
actors in the best light—Timmy being concerned that his
costume will upstage and unbalance him. Long, earnest talk
about him feeling scattered, drained, not knowing who he is,
lots of negativity surfacing. I urged meditation; we talked
about gardening, weeding, and "the daily renewal of character."[24] And I reminded him of how beloved he is by the company and how he deserves to experience himself the way
everybody else does. "I'm so lucky to have you," he said.
"You haven't had me," I thought, but spoke not.

At return, Trevor started work on the through line of
Act Two, summoning us all back on stage to become

[24] A phrase from the I Ching to which the requirements
of weeding always seem germane.

immersed in Old Deut's meditation, "The Moments of Happiness." Very beautiful inner focus work, culminating in the first group singing of "Memory"—still, lyrical, hushed, and tremendously moving—and out of this comes Gus. Ken Page and I found a beautiful moment—rooted in our long-ago mirror exercise—when Old D. chooses Gus to come forward. The number itself went very well for a first exposure, though, since the company was all arranged behind me, no one but the stage managers and swings could see my face (and Betty B., who watched from the side and said it was beautiful). By the end I was really drained—the concentration and vulnerability really take a lot.

At day's end, we were told that Willie had had successful microsurgery, that he would be able to dance again, but it would be months before he could return to the show.[25] Everyone groaned, even though we could hardly have expected otherwise. Then we emptied our lockers and turned in the keys: our last day in the rehearsal hall! Hard to believe.

Timmy and I hopped a cab up to the Avedon studio on 75th Street for our *Vogue* photo call. There was a table spread with food and drink and venerable Leo Lerman himself to welcome us. Ken P., Betty, Terry, Cynthia, and Donna soon followed. Noshing, schmoozing, etc. Finally Napier

[25] In fact it was a full year. He played Skimbleshanks in the first National Tour, which opened in Boston in the fall of 1983.

wants to get the show on the road. Timmy, Cynthia and Terry are the first shift. Makeup and wig people swarming over them like bees in a hive. Then I'm up. It takes hours, but finally we're ready. Timmy, Terry, Donna, and I stare and swarm over each other in a full-length mirror, just as Dick Avedon arrives. He loves the image of the four of us overlapping and decides to base his composition on it. Everybody looks fabulous. The makeups leave us nearly unrecognizable, yet they're remarkably expressive. I feel several levels deeper into Gus, who looks rather like Richard Kiley as Don Quixote. Timmy is elegance itself in his bead-riddled black satin, Cynthia the most pristine and precious white kitten, Ken sage and reverent, Betty downright Zola-esque in her faded glad rags. Avedon clumps us together and begins to play with composition and focus. He's like a playful little kid, bursting with enthusiasm, full of ideas and appreciation. "You're beautiful, beautiful. White cat, can you lift your breasts?" At one point he asks Napier, "Is Steve overacting?" "He has a tendency to overact," says Nape. They're a perfect match. We switch from a vertical to a horizontal position, all of us sprawled over each other on the floor. It's obviously a great picture but hard to maintain. Groans and giggles. Throughout, Avedon keeps up his flow of wit, good cheer, and joyous effervescence. Mastery in action. At last we break and gather at a restaurant for beer and munchies, exchanging theater stories and feeling very convivial, indeed. Napier pays with a $100 bill.

This morning I slept in. What a luxury (the shape of things to come)—and about 12:45 I ran into Harry approaching the Winter Garden stage door. "It's come to this!" Checked out my dressing room—smaller than the one at the Minskoff, and on the top floor, but with a window! I'm lucky to have it. The company collected downstairs, marveling over the vastness and complexity of the outsize collage that reaches out and absorbs the entire house. Strings of Christmas lights crisscross the ceiling beneath multiple panels of star motifs. Teapots, bicycles, empty food boxes and cans, plates, eggshells, fish skeletons, saucers, toothpaste tubes—it would be impossible to catalogue every visible object—not even Napier knows. Trevor's first words when we assembled were, "Well, I suppose first we must all acknowledge that John Napier is a genius." A round of substantive applause. Then we toured the set, discovering all the nooks, crannies, manhole covers, and recesses through which we can enter the scene. Back in the house, we watched the hydraulics operate, as Napier clambered and leaped over every surface like a mountain goat. The car boot opening, the Macavity light show, the Heaviside Layer Journey and finally, the ship. We all gasped, shrieked, and clapped, and at last TN said, "You remember what I said the first day about our sense of innocence. Now that you've had your own reaction to the set, you'll understand that one of the main concerns of this show is to allow the audience the experience of becoming like little children again." My eyes were filled with tears—Tim's also. One of the most moving incidents of the entire process.

We began to work through the show, placing the numbers on the set, adapting to the sight lines of this remarkably wide, wraparound space. Traffic problems getting up the stairs to the tire, entrances, etc. We're really working!

Friday 10 Sept Day 29

Ran into Treat Williams on the way to rehearsal. Brought him in for a look at the set, which blew him away. Broadway has simply never seen anything like it. Trevor set to work at once staging "The Naming," directing everyone to their positions in the house. He cautioned that the time when we're watching solo Cynthia from the aisles is crucial: people will begin to analyze the costume components, etc., unless we maintain an acute and hypnotic concentration. "You've got to look like nothing anyone has ever seen before, which is easy if you're Steve Hanan, but for the rest of us . . ."

We continue placing numbers. Terry is phenomenal as the Tugger, leaping all over from height to height, blazing with energy. I feel rather tentative as Bustopher, although having a house to play to is beginning to oil my instincts. Trevor says, "I think it's fabulous that you're doing Bustopher with no rehearsal, and I promise you we'll take some time to work on it." "Mungojerrie" is marvelous. Tim puts it over superbly, and René and Christine's teamwork is a joy. At the end, Gillie clambers up the ladder to the stage right proscenium box and decides that's where she wants Tim to finish. So he does—looking great. The number will be a big hit for sure.

At day's end, the boat is lowered and Trevor contemplates it. Suddenly Gillie leaps onto the deck, bounds up to the top level and hurtles back down to stage level in four antelopean jumps. Trevor and I stare at her in disbelief.

11 Sept Day 30

The morning's work (actually it starts at 1) is placing the Jellicle Ball. Long painstaking work. Then, at last, Gillie puts the tag on it, everyone breaking out randomly into one final trick: back flips, handsprings, walkovers, double *tours*—whatever they can do. It's spectacularly chaotic but I'm somewhat skeptical about how it will work. We stage the few remaining blank spaces, such as the kidnapping of Old Deut, where I appear at the high upstage left ramp and must scramble down with René and Herman and Kenny, across the tire and out the down right ramp. Don't feel too secure about the jumping, but I'll just need to practice. We block the end of the show, from the acceptance of Grizabella, which is intensely powerful. Cynthia (and others) are in tears, Betty can barely get the words out. Trevor gives Gus a long cross to be the first adult to salute her, and it's a thrilling moment. The whole company sends her waves of love and respect as she prepares to ascend. Even without the machinery it feels as if the heavens are opening. Utterly extraordinary. Magical. Transforming. All petty grievances—the problems of dancing on the rake, the raggedness of patterns in the Ball (which I noted unmistakably from my high perch) are wiped away for the moment.

After dinner, we have what Trevor calls a "stagger-through." Actually it goes very smoothly. The first act flies by, and we're all astonished to learn it only ran 62 minutes. The second act is done without Growltiger, which we still haven't staged, but doing Gus on stage for the first time leaves me utterly exhausted. The most intense acting concentration I've ever done. Onstage and in the house there is much dabbing of eyes, yet I feel the real cathartic payoff of the end has eluded me—as it must until Growltiger is incorporated. "Skimbleshanks," like "Gumbie," seems much too long (Reed doesn't make it work the way Willie did, and he's still halfway between his own characterization and a Willie imitation). Donna is fabulous in "Macavity"—how can anyone so cool be so hot?—and then we are given our first glimpse of the Mistoffelees dance. Tim is simply wonderful, but along about the pirouettes he begins to give out and has to walk through the rest of the number. We're all rooting for him (his mock-embarrassed gesture at "seven kittens" is a huge laugh moment), but he's clearly at the end of his stamina and most distressed. The rest of the show, from Dawn onwards, is superb, moving, exhilarating, and uplifting. The feeling on stage is just fabulous. Trevor and Gillie come forward and we all sit on the stage. He says: "Two things are obvious: you are a wonderful company, so wonderful together that our success is assured. Second, the star of the show *is* the company. One cannot help but be emotionally pulled in by the quality of your work together." But there's still much to achieve and particularly developing stamina is crucial for everyone. He warns of the dangers coming with tech week, but his mood is clearly exhilarated—though his natural buoyancy hasn't been much in evidence since we entered the theater. He's not exactly nervous, but there's a tension about him that actually makes him quite electric. He's working quickly, being more authoritarian ("I want quiet, and I want it *NOW!*"), rationing his energy, juggling a million variables, and everybody's faith in him is still strong. In fact, it's a remarkable demonstration of grace under pressure.

Anyhow, everyone watching seems quite impressed with the run-through. Napier tells me, "The two parts I was most afraid of not working in America were Bustopher and Gus, and I don't want to swell your head, but I've got to say you're superb." Fred Nathan[26] calls me brilliant. It's all very exciting, but I won't be happy till I know what Growltiger's demands are.

[26] The show's publicist.

6th WK

Monday 13 Sept — Day 31

Wonderful day off. Timmy came out to Rowayton[27] and we all drove to Edith's and a perfect beach day. He enchanted everyone and vice versa. ("You sure have a yummy body," said Laurie, with her inimitable directness.) But he's really worried about the Mistoffelees dance and concerned that fifteen lbs. of battery-packed costume can only make it worse. But Matt arrives Thursday from California and I'm sure that will give him some extra zest.

Costume fitting at 12:30. The sleek black & orange Macavity Henchman—masked terrorist. Then the Gus robe, which blanketing the woolen Growltiger tunic is like noon in Panama—but it looks fabulous.

At the theater a day of tech work. The lights are marvelous. It all looks too magical for words. But the constant stop-and-start is grueling, as always, and still no Growltiger. I am beginning to get antsy. Well, at least they put a carpet in my dressing room, and wardrobe moved in today led by the irrepressible, Felliniesque Adelaide Laurino. Truly all will be well.

---

[27] Home of a couple of married friends, Howard & Laurie, in Connecticut.

Tues 14 Sept Day 32

Walked in this morning and the boat was in place. "This can mean only one thing," I thought. Then it went up again. Trevor said we'd go on with teching "Tugger." "I see a lot of worried faces wondering when will we do Growltiger. But it's useless to do it until all the pieces are in place and we've decided to spend all of Saturday on it." His eyes met mine at that moment, and he saw my shock, disappointment, and fear. I've not felt so disheartened during the entire process, as I subsequently told Tim and Nancy Bell, the wonderful production assistant whose serene and loving presence I may not yet have noted in these pages. They urged me to ask TN for a pep talk, but before I had the chance to do so, he came over to me, reading me clearly, and with his arm around me said, "I can see how this could be worrying to you, but don't let it be. After all, what's the point?" He explained that Gillie and Andrew each wanted the other to produce first. "But we've made our commitment and it'll be kept." My mind continued to brood for a while, but basically I felt healed by his words.

We teched "Bustopher" and Trevor loved my perform-ance (Tim simply said, "You're great."), but I told him I always felt lost in the midst of it, without any clear prepara-tion. He gave me the image of a Tory MP coming out for the obligatory handshaking and baby kissing with the lower classes, cultivating the people they've been grinding down for centuries. "Yes my dear and how is the shopping? You say you've been eating beans? How delightful." The number proceeded to improve markedly. Then he prepared us for the Mungojerrie entrance. "You know how adults are when the theater lights do down,"—clearing his throat and miming the finicky assumption of over-earnest attentiveness—"but for children it's like this,"—miming wild excitement—"because the *lights are going down!*" It was one of his most effective communications. Also the number keeps getting better and better. René and Christine were in costume, looking sensational. We got up to the distribution of the Peke and Pollicle costumes—utterly hilarious. Then broke for dinner.

Herman and boy-René and I went to Popeye's and brought back a bunch of chicken to Ken Page's room and had a lovely time. Then we got to run "Pekes" with Ken Ard—Chocolate Box, as Gillie calls him—emerging from the star trap. It really looks as if the stage is vomiting him forth: one of the most astonishing effects I've ever seen. We got midway through the Ball, falling short of Trevor's aim of going at least to the intermission. After the break, Tim stayed to run his solo. He was marvelous, but midway through landed badly on his left ankle. Everyone froze, but he walked it off and continued finishing superbly. Everyone cheered. He is a star dancer of the highest degree. Many of his moves drew gasps, even from us who know him. Then he hurriedly put some ice on the ankle.

While I changed, the boat was dropped in, including the wonderful painted curtain with flapping seagull. I finally got to present my walk-the-plank mime to Trevor, Gillian, and Andrew. "I'm sure this is going to be outrageous," TN said, and afterwards, "It certainly was," and though they all found it very funny, it was deemed too long and stylistically wrong for what they're planning there. But he said he'd use some of the beats in it, told me they all loved me, and ushered me swiftly out to put the piece together. I said good night to Tim, who couldn't relevé on the injured ankle but doesn't seem overly concerned, and I told him how proud I was to have seen him break through his perceived limitations. He was happy to have done it all, and it felt real good. Amen, and may his ankle be fully operative *tout de suite*.

Wed 15 Sept Day 33

We began at once with the Ball and Gillie put Anna and me into it at last (or rather took us out, as we leave the stage after a brief sojourn and return on the high ramp just for the very end—some new steps to learn). Tim came in late and joined right in—evidently it's just a mild sprain, thank the Lord. Janet and girl-René are very unhappy with the Ball; they can't stop moaning during it, and it seems as much bad attitude as physical difficulty (or does each create the other?). But from the upper vantage point it's certainly looking better.

We moved right on to the second act. Gus went well, and

this time the boat was lowered. (TN to Bonnie on clearing her prop: "Take up your can and walk, as the Bible says.") I turned around and was amazed to see it—romantic back-lighting and all. "Look what the cat dragged in," I blurted into my mike (yes, we're wearing them now), and broke myself up. Then it ascended again and I did Gus' final exit, not very inspired. Trevor came up on stage, hugged me close and whispered, "I already know you're one of the three most inventive people in the world; you don't have to prove it to me. What I want you to prove is that you can be simple." I did it again with almost no gesture but still felt there was nothing there. But I know it'll be fine after I've played the actual Growltiger sequence.

Long time spent on building the Skimbleshanks train. Mucho logistics, but when at last completed, it looks fantas-tic. Another Napier triumph—but I'm glad not to have to assemble it. I next appear as a Macavity Henchman[28] and my insecurity in jumping from car hood to tire is sufficient that Trevor and Gillie reblock me to slide down the chute instead. I feel very awkward learning the hang of it, but at last I do. Not my favorite moment in the show, though Gillie's Cagney image is fun to play with and anyway, my face is covered (there's an actor for you).

---

[28] One of three masked thugs who help to abduct Old Deuteronomy.

I break early to get made up for the *Life* shoot. Napier essays a whole new look, this time one that will work for both Gus and Growltiger. It's fabulous, we both acknowledge that this is the one to stay with. Others drift in after 9:30 to be made up. I leave and visit with Betty. We have this deep conversation about love, romance, attachment, the supposed but imperceptible benefits of celibacy, etc. till we notice how absurd we look waxing profound in our cat outfits. We laugh and cuddle and Betty suggests we meditate. We sit together in the darkened dressing room as the sound of preparation hums around us. It's very peaceful and lovely to be with her. I finally open my eyes and she does so shortly thereafter. We gaze at each other with free and undemanding love. It's beautiful.

The limo comes, complete with TV. Half a dozen flash cameras are ranged at the stage door (it's begun). Betty, Ken Ard, Timmy, and I ride down in one. Several new looks tonight. Hoshour, Mercado, Harry G—all great. Anna in her sea of orange fringe. Timmy a-twinkle with lights. But the hit is my inflatable tunic, which nets me twenty minutes with the camera right off. Fred[29] warns of mutiny if the group picture doesn't happen right away, so we do that one and I get to leave. Home by limo at 2:30 A.M., passing my old street-singing corner in SoHo! How the world doth turn.

[29] Publicist Fred Nathan

Thurs 16 Sept Day 34

First time with the orchestra. The bleary-eyed survivors of
last night (Tim and Anna got home at 5!) drag themselves
into Carroll Studios. Four synthesizers, three cellos, and
more wind instruments than I've ever seen. Stanley launches
the overture and we go crazy. What a hot band! Tight and
juicy. Everybody wakes up. "Jellicle Songs" is fabulous—you
can't help but get up and boogie. Each number is another
gem of arranging. "Gumbie" has the authentic big band 40s
swing sound. "Tugger" is Otis Redding funk-rock. The eerie
synthesizer wind slides of "Grizabella," "Bustopher's"
sonorous Buckingham Palace brasses. Then "Mungojerrie,"
building from tick-tock wind-up doll playfulness to a full-
scale Broadway jazz finish. What a showstopper it will be.
"Old Deut," "Pekes and Pollicles," and finally the Ball, which
electrifies! The dance-band sound—especially the salsa seg-
ments—is irresistible. Whether the audience can remain
seated is certainly in doubt. The brilliant inventiveness and
power of David Cullen's arrangements is matched by the pre-
cision and flair of the band. Act One is a triumph.

Act Two—Gus. I face outwards and take the opportunity
to play, at last, to the company. Between their nurturing
faces and my simplicity quest, something wonderful happens.
The number is better than it has ever been. Bonnie kisses me
as she takes her seat and everyone applauds at the end. I
feel like I've nailed it.

The remainder of the act goes superbly. "Skimbleshanks" perks. "Macavity" sizzles, and the Mistoffelees dance is dazzling, with a trap solo during the pirouettes. "Memory" is gorgeous. Just before the Heaviside ascent and "Addressing" I feel my lack of sleep overcoming me, and heads are nodding all around the room. But the final moments are so galvanizing and sumptuous that everyone's full energy is restored. Cheers abound.

Trevor gives credit to Stanley and David, then reminds cast and orchestra that we must always maintain the sense of cooperation and mutual respect we shared today, as we are and must remain "each other's lifeline to the show." Then he adds, "I don't know what the appropriate time to say this would be, but since it must be said, I'll do it now: I feel that this is one of the greatest scores ever written for a musical." Cheers and bravos for the genius of Andrew and we break for a Friday day off, to return on Saturday for Growltiger (at LAST!) and 10 out of 12 week.[30]

Saturday 18 Sept Day 35 Rosh Hashanah

I'd have to say today was the greatest day of my professional life. (Prepared for by a visit to Long Beach yesterday.

[30] For final tech & dress rehearsals, Actors Equity permits a limited number of 12-hour work days, with a two-hour lunch break.

Gorgeous weather, I swam in the ocean, and had lovely heart-to-heart talks with each parent separately about how excited I am about my prospects. "Is that what you want to be, a star?" asked Dad, with a wonderful mixture of pride and affirmation. I sang for them and left in a glow of deep and well-shared love. Then this morning Barbara Somerfield called to forecast great results from the dynamic Mars-Uranus conjunction currently transiting my natal Venus, then going to my ascendant, with Jupiter repeating the same pattern from mid-November all through 1983; most felicitous, as long as the high mental energy doesn't force the body faster than it can go.)

Anyway, the morning began with a warm-up and the Ball. I'm getting better at the newly added end section, but still not perfect. Then the boat descended and Gillie taught the Siamese attackers their toasting-fork dance. At last she put me and Bonnie into it—lots of dirty fighting and mock-heroics. By dinner I was exhausted, but I had also had more fun than any time since Day One. As I left to eat, I stopped Trevor and said, "A play is play,"[31] and he gave me the most warm and loving look.

But the real fun started after dinner. The release of the crew from the hold, their sudden demise (hilarious), and

[31] Last sentence of Peter Brook's classic The Empty Space

Griddlebone's flight.[32] Then we went back to do the opening, figuring how to get the crew working on the boat before it descends, establishing my relationship with them (Timmy is a scream as the little wimp and Harry, Reed, Terry, and Hector all are great). We work so well together that it takes no time to get things going. I'm inventing like mad, really going for it (as Napier urged me this morning). Total romantic excess—but Gillie and Trevor keep reminding me that there are boundaries, that I need to stay in control, play genuine machismo without becoming fey or commenting. We get through the aria (Trevor brilliantly solves the concertina disposal—a crew hand emerges from the hold), Bonnie and I having a wonderful time together, me turning on this intense sexual heat and she both turned on and embarrassed. The aria-duet knocks 'em dead ("Can you believe we're standing alone on a Broadway stage and doing this?" she says) and then we hook it up with the previous work. Girl-René tells me "You'll get a Tony for this." I promise her

32 The Growltiger sequence is the dream of Gus: up & down the bridge of a theatrically hokey pirate ship prowls the dread Growltiger, terrorizing & then dismissing his crew when the luscious Lady Griddlebone appears, wrapped in a white feather boa. After an aria of seduction they are on the verge of cat-coition when the ship is overrun by Siamese pirates. Griddlebone flees, Growltiger fights single-handedly, is eventually subdued, dies noisily & then rises again only to walk the plank. All vanishes & Gus is left alone with his memory.

dinner at Lutece if she's right. Boy-René pats my fake paunch, "You're fabulous. You're so funny." Out in the house, Cameron, Andrew, and the others are blissful. David Hersey: "You're outrageous." Candy: "You're wonderful." And on and on. Even though the death combat, wounding, and plank-walk remain to be done, it's been a phenomenal day, much accomplished, myself at the point of total physical and vocal exhaustion but exhilarated, happy, totally fulfilled, and immensely grateful to God for the life within me.

Sunday 19 Sept Day 36

Dress rehearsal. Everything and everyone look great but create a host of problems. First, the Gumbie costume change. Both Anna and the beetles tattoo are late. Everything stops and we work it out, Trevor and John in tandem patient and cool and totally in command. But the work goes very slowly. People can't see out of the beetles' helmets, or their wigs are crushed. Timmy's dislike of his costume creates a palpable field around him. But the moment the wings open is incredible. More trouble with Tugger quick changes. Everybody scrambling around the wings with tap shoes, etc. My dresser, Steve Smith, is gentle and solicitous and most helpful. We do the Bustopher change—only the makeup at this point—after the dinner break (Joanne brings back food for those of us who don't want to change to go out). No problems—but I can't fit into the Pekes and Pollicles foot cartons with my own shoes on. So it goes.

The Rumpus Cat costume drives everyone wild with its airbrushed musculature clinging exquisitely to Ken Ard's. The Ball goes great in the costumes—brings down the small attending house. We move to the second act and everything is fucked. I can't make the bandanna work for the Gus-to-Growltiger change, which means I can't get the robe off in time to throw under the boat. Napier immediately locates the problem and solves it. The Siamese and Raffish Crew masks mangle everyone's wigs and makeup. Trevor cuts Growltiger after a few bars in, which is just as well as I'm ominously certain that in the heat and pressure of the costume I'd never get through it. It's scary and I'm exhausted. Tim is furious, quoting Gillie as saying that everything that made the show great in London was gone. The humanity is submerged under the weight of special effects. A palace revolt is brewing, but I know only that I'm exhausted and alarmed and discouraged.

7th WK: Previews to Begin!

Monday 20th Sept   Day 37

Day starts with just Steve Gelfer and me setting the Growltiger-Genghis sword fight. It's wonderful. Then my preposterous death scene after being ignominiously stabbed in the tush. The company joins us and we work through to the finish (minus the plank that is still not ready)—Gillie is incredibly fast and the end product is marvelous—funny, melodramatic, absurd, and thrilling. We run the whole number—I sail through the aria, and though just before the end I've no clue where my energy is coming from, I persist and make it through. It will be fantastic—if I can do it in the costume, which weighs over thirty pounds!

We finish in time for the break, and Michael and Patricia[33] meet me for dinner. It's great to see them and they pick up instantly on my exhilaration from the afternoon's work. Much encouragement and support. We meet Tim and Matt on the way back and plug in the Rev. Terry connection. Then it's dress and makeup time again. The first act goes without a hitch. I find an emotional depth at the end of Gus that nearly swamps me, but I ride it out and

[33] Visiting from California, also students of Terry Cole Whittaker.

turn it into joy. Very powerful. Then silence. Trevor comes on stage and asks could I bear it if we skipped Growltiger and teched it tomorrow. So we do. He starts teching Skimbleshanks and I go up to fit the Bustopher coat. I'm called down urgently to run the Macavity Henchman change. Once again out of the whiskers and wig and again back into them. Tempers are short—even Herman gets pissed. I accost Napier over the absence of glow tape on the high stage left ramps and he sternly requests that I stay cool, he'll provide whatever I need, "but don't come at me like that." Lots of pressure. Ken Ard pissed because his dance gets bumped in favor of teching Mistoffelees, and Tim—giving his absolute best—cannot dance in the costume. It's so sad to see him try and fail, but Gillie flocks to him and it's assured that Napier will redo the costume so it can be removed in time for the heavy dancing, but still make its splendid light-up effect. Afterwards Tim and Matt (who's wonderful) and I go out to eat. We confess to each other our intuition that we'll be "competing" for the same Tony. We laugh, admit that we'd happily see the other win (though not so happily lose) and declare our sense of privilege at being nominated in the other's company. So now all we need is the nomination!

Tuesday 21st Sept Day 38

So, one day it's Tonys and the next, it's chopped liver. Hard day teching Growltiger, but finally we ran it, including the costume. Trevor asked me if I wanted to try the jump, off the plank and into a netful of mattresses. At first I said no, the costume was ordeal enough, but then changed my mind for the sake of getting the Gus return right. So without a practice run, right on cue, I jumped onto the mattresses. Piece of cake—and I got through the whole number without collapsing (till I hit the wings). So that was a great achievement.

After dinner, Nicole joined me, looking wonderful as ever, and we in turn joined Timmy and Matt and their friend Nancy from San Francisco. Then we went for (and achieved) a full run-through! We got through it, tire, cherrypicker, and all,[34] but I felt rather down—the small house we had applauded several numbers, but not Gus. Timmy—even in the lighter costume—couldn't complete the dance. Steve Smith—my gentle and solicitous dresser—assured me the number was fine, I was terrific, etc., but it just isn't working right yet.

34 The most famous of Cats' effects, as Grizabella rides up to Heaven.

Wed 22 Sept Day 39

Major change in Growltiger. Trevor removed the return-of-the-crew section. Now it goes straight from the surprise attack into G-bone's flight and the fight. Far more effective. Melodramatic tableaux, one after another.

Prior to this, we met at the Bennett Studios at noon to do some cleaning. Very useful to be back in that environment as a reminder of the first nurturing stages of the process. Also Trevor took me out of the Macavity Henchmen sequence, which reduced me to jelly last night—going from the exhaustion of Gus-Growltiger into that costume change sopping wet, peeling the hair and then climbing the spiral staircase and running down the set nearly finished me. So that's done with, thank God.

About sixty to seventy people were invited to the final dress. In spite of many technical fluffs it was mainly there and I think we're a hit. The spectacle gets great response, the Ball was a tremendous showstopper, and there's other surefire hit numbers. Bustopher got lots of laughs—the costume is great and I ate my tail to great response—and Gus was also a smash. Growltiger went well in the main, but there's too much time after the Gus return and so the ending was bollixed (or as Trevor prefers, quoting Beckett, "banjaxed"), and I think people aren't following all the narrative. But it will come together—and tonight I didn't need to collapse afterward!

Tim still had to mark sections of his dance. He's scared and worried and his brilliance isn't coming across. I hope they have the sense to adapt the dance to his own skills. But the audience was wild at the end and we all hugged each other and Trevor on stage, there being as yet no curtain call. Matt was most enthusiastic, predicting confidentially that I would walk away with the notices. And yet I'm dissatisfied— there's lots more acting values to find and I want this show to be Tim's door to stardom. Also I want the fuzzy narrative sections to be cleared up.

Thur 23 Sept Day 40 — First Preview

More changes in Growltiger—group lines have now been spread among individuals, which should clarify the story and also add more acting moments for me and Bonnie. Other small changes throughout the show, new mikes, lighting cues, etc. Trevor's last words before the break were a reminder of how much we have to give the audience tonight—"make your offering and have fun." He remains the essence of calm and patience, despite all the new stuff for tonight—the light-up overture glasses[35] and the outrageously complex curtain call (I wish Gillie could take it easy some-times).

[35] Worn by the cast as we ran around the darkened auditorium.

Matt, Tim, and I go to dinner. Tim remarks that I seem quite calm. "Actually, it's paralysis." Truth is it hasn't really hit me that we're playing a preview tonight, though toward the end of dinner I experience some flutters. By 7:15, I'm getting into wig and makeup, having finally mastered the painting of my own face. At Fifteen Minutes, Steve helps me into the costume (maneuvering around the huge bundle of black, gold, and white balloons Greg Gorden has brought), and I'm ready with time to spare at Places. Everyone wishing each other "Merde" and "Break a paw." The atmosphere is marvelous, electric. The overture begins, we steal into the house and blink our cat-eyes on and off. It's hard to gauge the response because the shock of people being in every seat is so great. Overture gets a great hand and off we go. The opening is marvelous and applause begins just before the moment when I cut it off. "Naming" is great, it's wonderful playing it to real people. "Gumbie" gets a great hand, the first such opportunity of the night, so much that the play-off music before "Tugger" seems an endless stage wait. I make my change and get big laughs on Bustopher, and a hand at the end—even without a button. Timmy plays his embarrassment over the tacky, wind-out-of-a-sheet Mungojerrie entrance and gets a solid laugh. I give him the prearranged signal (polishing my monocle to mean "make it a joy-offering to God) and he perks up and sells the number to great applause. With the Macavity scare I'm off again for another quick change, returning for "Pekes and Pollicles," which gets a tremendous hand. The Ball brings the house down, though during its length, there doesn't seem much audience involvement. Curious.

Act Two. Off we go. Gus gets a hand at the end of Bonnie's first segment, again at mine, and again at the finish. The costume change gets a hand. The boat gets a hand. The aria gets a hand. They go quite mad for it, though my re-entry as Gus seems anticlimactic and the exit applause is less than I'd wanted. The train gets a hand and "Macavity" stops the show. Tim makes his rope entrance without the light-jacket and does beautifully, though he improvises in some places to conceal his fatigue. Betty wows 'em with "Memory," and the tire effect is sensational. By the curtain call, the entire house is on its feet and everyone is ecstatic. Great joy backstage. Trevor, Andrew, and Cameron accost me to say that Growltiger never had anything like this effect in London. "I'd say it's been a very good night for you," Trevor says. I do feel terrific, though exhausted. Tim invites me to share some champagne Matt's brought. I meet Bob Duva, Tim's agent, who wants to talk with me at a later date (he's told René Ceballos that I'm a cinch for a Tony nomination). I get loaded and roll home after 2, to greet Cameron[36] with the news of our triumphant success.

36 Duncan, not Mackintosh, with whom I shared the loft in TriBeCa.

Friday 24 September   Day 41

Noon rehearsal. Trevor is very happy but still sees much
work to be done. "But I promised myself that I'd get
through this day without bringing down that fucking boat!"
First we put a button on Bustopher, to hold for the
applause. I ask TN if we should cut the flower toss, since eating my tail seems to work better. "It works if you like that
sort of thing," he replies. Then Tim's Mungojerrie entrance
is re-staged with much more flair, cutting the sheet. Polish
here, there, and elsewhere. The performance is a $250/seat
Arts Council Benefit to a black-tie audience of deadly stiffs.
But they recognize Bustopher as one of their own and clap
vigorously. Growltiger wows them and I find it easier to do
each time. The performance is very good throughout,
despite the audience's dullness.

Saturday 25 September   Day 42

First two-show day. The matinee is very good. My bandanna
(newly snap-equipped) stays on throughout for the first
time, which helps me no end, especially in acting through to
the finish. Audiences are having a great time, in spite of the
lapses in continuity or excitement that are obviously occur-
ring. Much of the "plot" is incomprehensible, and yet it
doesn't seem to matter.

Everyone's tired for the evening show, but it's a good one nevertheless. Timmy, continuing a trend begun in the afternoon, is relaxing and being ever more outrageous, sensual, feeling himself up, parking his tail between his teeth, having fun. Growltiger keeps getting better. I'm developing the stamina to keep everything controlled and less haphazard (Gillie asks if I'd mind prolonging the sword fight since it's such a crowd-pleaser, and I assent), though it still pisses me off that I can't hear the roar of applause at the end because of the quick change back to Gus. Timmy does his solo in the jumpsuit for the first time and though he's so tired that he's sloppy, the audience loves him. In fact there seems to be an established pattern that the heightened bursts of curtain-call applause go to him, Betty, Terry, and me.

Michael and Patricia and Nicole and Jim Latus come back afterwards (also Stockard Channing, to our mutual surprise), all loving the show and thrilled by my performance. They're all so proud of me. On to a party thrown by the producers for just the company at Sardi's upstairs. More fulsome praise from Gerry Schoenfeld, Cameron M, René Ceballos' family, and Michael from the original London company ("You stole the show."). I spot Trevor in his pink sport coat and say, "You're wearing your Raquel Welch jacket." He rubs my bewigged pate and replies, "You're wearing your photo-call hair." The food is sensational and varied and the party is just what we all need.

Mon 27 Sept Day 43

Rehearsal at the downtown studio again. Nice to be away from the theater. Gillie does some tightening of the Ball. She is the most incredible workhorse—on and on and on with unflagging spirits. Trevor also seems to have regained his energy level and is quite buoyant. I'm released early and go to the gym for a sauna, where I'm amazed to discover that I've *gained* 10 lbs. since rehearsals began!

7 o'clock call at the theater. I can't really comprehend that we're performing again: somehow it seems as if last week's four previews were a quirky experiment interrupting the rehearsal process. But no, we have an audience, and a good one, though the day off has sapped my Growltiger stamina and the number exhausts me as thoroughly as last week—but I add some things at the end, chiefly Growltiger getting religion and praying for forgiveness before his leap— the last hokey touch, heartily endorsed by Trevor. After the show, Marilyn Redfield, her mother, and some friends, and Don Correia come back, all fulsome with praise and congratula- tions. Dan Marcus says "You're as good as you think you are."

Tuesday 28 Sept Day 44

Timmy had a private rehearsal with Gillie at the Minskoff, and when he came in to do his dance, he was sensational. She's simplified it and set it up better so that his jetés get off the ground, for one thing. Everyone applauded. There was a long session on the Ball, which David Hersey re-lit extensively while Trevor talked at length with me about Gus. SIMPLICITY again. "But I'm using all the restraint I know how," I said, ". . . well, nearly," which gave him occasion for one of those great ironic smiles I've come to love. I asked him to get specific and at last he zeroed in on "swung on the bell" and "never get trained," as places where too much strength was coming through, foreshadowing Growltiger. Older, frailer. And still he's not satisfied with "moment of mystery," or the reaction to Steve Gelfer's shadowy Siamese that Dan Marcus liked so much. "You try to play two things at the same time, and my job is to get you to pick one."

The performance is good. Already we can distinguish different audience types. Tonight they're clappers but not laughers. But Growltiger is easier this time and Tim's dance is wonderful, earning Bravos. I wear my Growltiger bandanna for the curtain call and receive a noticeably higher level of cheers.

Wednesday 29 Sept Day 45

A great matinee. Not just blue-hairs, but lotsa kids and young grown-ups—any chance to see the show. Good evening show but tiring. Props offered me a boutonnière made of cabbage leaves to eat as Bustopher. I try it in the wings. It could be very funny but it's too hard to chew. So back to the tail. René Wiegert conducts—beautifully—while Stanley sits in the house, seeing the show at last.[37] At intermission he broadcasts: "This is your former TV personality. The show looks wonderful and sounds wonderful. You're all to be congratulated." The Big S!

Matt and Tim to dinner afterward and get to meet Cameron D at last. A wonderful evening together, but it is curtailed by Tim's having an 11 A.M. rehearsal tomorrow morning!

Thurs 30 Sept Day 46

More Growltiger changes, shortening the first Siamese chase sequence. While Gillie teaches the Siamese, Trevor takes me and Bonnie aside and works beat by beat through the seduction scene, sharpening the focus on Griddlebone's ambivalence ("Stop it, I like it."). As usual, he poses goals and leaves

37 The Cats orchestra was housed backstage left, and the cast watched the conductor on monitors along the balcony rail.

it to us to offer the methods of solution, and we come up with some wonderful new stuff. Stanley suggests that at last night's viewing he found Gus too virile and the voice too strong. Trevor notes that this is on a first viewing and consequently worth attending to. Must create wider contrast between Gus and Growltiger.

Gillie adds some beats to the sword fight and we run the ending several times. At last I get to play with different ideas on walking the plank and select and polish without the pressure of performance. Finally we add the technical run of the new disappearing mast, so that moment at last makes sense. Four and a half hours on Growltiger! I'm bushed. The last half hour spent rehearsing a new entrance for Tim—the rope comes down while the chorus sings, instead of on a drum roll. Looks much better.

Tonight's audience is very dull. I'm so exhausted from rehearsal and running to the chiropractor on meal break, I can't hit the B-flat during my intermission warm-up. But Growltiger turns the audience around, they howl with laughter, the note comes through by the grace of God, and the rest of the act is turned around. But I come home so tired I can hardly find my way to bed.

Friday, 1st October Day 47

It's actually October! This process, by every indication one of the major turning points in my life, that began with a fresh-from-Jamaica audition on 2 February, has now reached the month of its culmination. I'm utterly amazed at how fast the time has gone, at how much I've grown under Trevor's direction, at how the audiences have been responding, and at how close I've come to the fulfillment of my oldest and deepest dream. I'm on the verge of tears all the time, especially when I see anybody old and frail and forlorn to remind me of Gus. Walking down Church Street to the gym (I'm not called till 2:30), it suddenly hits me how to play the last lines after Gus' return: internally, as if the audience weren't there, closing my eyes on "made history" and *then* becoming aware of people when I re-open my eyes, and leaving in embarrassment. I'm sure this will work for me and provide what Trevor wants.

At the theater, "Gumbie" has been shortened; Tim and Cynthia's duet is gone (to their delight). Trevor spots me in the darkened house and says, "Where'd you spring from?" "The brain of Zeus—full grown," I reply. "I believe it," says he. "I believe you do," I respond. The afternoon's off to a great start. Trevor works on the train assemblage. Tim complains of soreness and I offer him a massage. He declines and then impulsively changes his mind. I give him a long slow massage in the aisle of the theater, releasing some knots in his lower back and shoulders. I'm enjoying the suppleness of his muscles and he's moaning and the whole process is deeply hypnotic, when I hear Trevor call my name. He wants to segue into "Skimbleshanks" from the final Gus moment. I skip onto the stage and play the moment with eyes closing and re-opening. It goes well but TN complains of my rushing the exit cross. I try again and this time it's perfect. Afterwards Nancy Bell says it was the best I've ever done it. "Do it that way tonight and I'll be in puddles on the floor." As it happens in performance, the Growltiger sequence makes the tag work even better. The applause is fuller and warmer than ever before, and a man in the stage left seat block whispers, "Bravo," as I pass. I've got it! And later there's a note from Nancy on my dressing room door, "Puddles and puddles!"

Sat 2 October Day 48

Great, great matinee show. The last Gus moment works again. Tim Hunter[38] and Cindy attend; they are rapturous at the end. Howard and Laurie join us for Japanese food. *Tex* has just made a hit at the NY Film Festival and opened at Cinema One. I recollect the occasion in August 1969 when I told Tim I'd race him to the top. "I guess it's a draw," I said.

[38] My freshman roommate at Harvard; "Tex" was his professional debut as a director.

Howard reckons that Tim has beat me by a week. Howard and Laurie return to my dressing room and give me foot massages. They stop by to give greeting to Timmy on their way out.

The evening is as bad as the matinee was good. Typical Saturday night on Broadway—overfed, drunk, and somnolent. Gus gets none of its subtle laughs. Growltiger is a smash, though, and the quick change is rapid enough for me to get on stage in time to hear the applause. Jim Mulkin comes back to say that I and the show are great—but somewhere before "Heaviside Layer" I've pulled a neck muscle and can hardly turn my head. Damn.

9th WK

Monday 4 Oct Day 49

We convene in the house with Trevor at noon, Gillie nowhere in sight. He announces his intention of re-exploring the values we found at the very beginning of rehearsals, and the whole afternoon is spent working with him in top form. For an hour he gives notes, riffling through four or five days worth of foolscap. Upon giving me a note to cut the "explanatory" gesture on "Luna," he adds, "And I'm saying this in front of witnesses: No. Very clever—No." He gets back to the original essence of the process, his special concern being that it takes the whole first act and intermission to warm up the audience to what we're doing. What can we do to make them join us earlier on? How to switch from the arrogance and aloofness of the opening to an invitation to participate with us? He invites everyone's feedback and a great group discussion occurs, as in the early days (but with everyone speaking more effectively and briefly). I throw out my image of a remote tribe being visited by 1500 National Geographic photographers. Just before the break, Trevor confides this: "You must remember what the greatest power in the theater is. It has nothing to do with sets and special effects. It's what's going on in your minds, and how that affects the minds of the audience."

He talks about the falling off of spontaneity since we began technical work. "There is no more inventive group of people working together in theater anywhere on the planet than you. (*looking around*) I really mean that. You must find ways of reasserting that." I ask about pulling focus and he offers the analogy to a concert pianist playing with right and left hands: one half of our "theater brain" is totally committed to representing a character in full; the other remains aware of the greater needs of the whole piece at any given moment. He gives unstintingly of the distillate of his wisdom all day: cutting the first Macavity entrance and sharpening the Old Deut kidnap to better set up the Macavity fight—which indeed draws great applause that evening. Inventing ways to play more fully and warmly and wittily to the audience in Act One. Bringing acting values to the fore as choreography recedes. It's really an amazing day, a great deal is accomplished—not the least being a renewal of our company feeling at its warmest and most creative. The audience in the evening is so-so (till the finale, of course), but we do a truly great show.

Tuesday 5 oct Day 50!

Music and staging brush-up at the Minskoff. We assemble at 1:00 to learn that the company has been cut from "Mungojerrie"—it's now just the threesome. Stanley polishes the ensemble in "Bustopher." Trevor discovers—after emphasizing the importance of projecting lyrics, the foundation of the show (perhaps because Valerie Eliot[39] is coming tonight)—that many people don't know what a "Brummel" means, so he clears that up. He takes me aside to say the accent has gotten too thick, then adds, "Your judgment is impeccable. Whenever you address a scene the first time, the accuracy of your judgment is astonishing. But it's in the development process that you sometimes stretch too far. (*Long pause.*) Enough said."

The performance is a benefit for the Actor's Fund. Great audience. The new "Mungojerrie" gets a much better hand.

[39] Widow of the show's author.

During Act One I get a flash to set up the hand-licking at the final Gus exit by introducing the gesture at the beginning before Bonnie sings. That, in combination with really fine playing, produces the greatest response the number has ever had. It's just fabulous (even though midway through Growltiger, my shoulders begin a second, accidental inflation, the pressure irresistibly mounting till my arms are nearly pinned down—then a couple of leaks mercifully relieve me in the nick of time) and I get a tremendous ovation at the bows.

Wed 6 oct Day 51

3 o'clock call. A pep talk from Trevor on the importance of critics' night. It's fine to be full of nervous excitement, to have a sense of great occasion, to reconnect to what first made us, as children, want to be actors: performing for people and having them say we're fabulous. We need only to avoid the pitfall of fear—since none of us has anything *to* fear. How do people win tennis championships, he asks. One point at a time. If something goes wrong, don't fixate on it, just keep moving and go for the next moment. As usual, he fills everyone with calm and confidence. Some minor restaging: cutting the final "Peke" bagpipe distraction, adding a company bow. Little bits here and there.

Tim and I dine at Iroha again. He's nervous and feeling off. Neither of us stops leg-shaking through the entire meal. Back to the theater, where I'm antsy to get underway with wig-prep and makeup. At last it's 7:15, and going through the by-now-familiar motions takes my mind off the special significance of this performance. Despite Trevor's warning that there'd be a large block of critics in the house whose presence would be not that of participants but of observers and assessors, the audience feels terrific and the show goes very well. Trevor's pre-show intercom message: "Savor the language, go for the dancing, and reach the audience." Tim stops by before his dance still feeling unwell. I sit him down to a long *trespasso*,[40] reminding him to soak up the overflow energy of a man who's just brought down the house. The light comes back in his eyes, the smile returns to his face, and he goes off to the number, which gets Bravos, and the company bow brings the entire house to its feet. An excellent perform-ance, perhaps our best to date, and everyone is pleased.

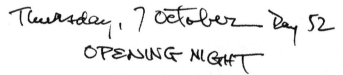

Thursday, 7 October — Day 52
OPENING NIGHT

I spend the day buying and wrapping gifts. Jay[41] arrives at 2:30 and it is blissful to be with him. Can a year have truly passed since our last meeting? It's amazing. He looks thinner, more mature, but still as gracious, intelligent, gentle, and

[40] Two-person meditation technique involving pro-longed eye contact.

[41] A sometime romantic interest from rural Connec-ticut.

irresistibly fine as ever. A wonderful auspice to have him
return today.

I reach the theater by 6. Everyone assembles to present
the company gifts. Backstage is crammed to the rafters with
flowers, telegrams, champagne. Buckets filled with cat food
boxes and Moet & Chandon line the stairs (gifts to the company from Ralston Purina). Every square foot of counter and
floor space in my room holds bouquets, long-stemmed roses,
champagne, cards, wires, packages, large and small. Everyone
is overwhelmed by the profusion of gifts and tokens.

Downstairs, Trevor proclaims that though he had no
speech prepared, he'll make one anyway: in spite of his claim
that last night was the really important night, he now states
that *tonight* is. There's applause for him, Gillie, Stanley, each
other. Declarations of love from everyone to everyone else.
The whoopingly ceremonial presentation of the Gypsy
Robe[42] to Bonnie Walker. Herman asks what's going on (like
the Simple Son at Passover, or the kitten he is), and up we
go to dress. Tim opens my gift and urges me to look at
mine: "You won't believe it." We've each given the other a

---

[42] A decades-old tradition: on the opening night of
every Broadway musical the Gypsy Robe is
presented to the oldest chorus member, who
to bring luck circles the stage wearing it. An
elaborate memento of the show is then
appliquéd to this bulky kimono (*Pirates* of
Penzance added a sea-blue train with toy
schooner floating behind), which vanishes
till the next opening night.

hunk of crystal. From Trevor, a bottle of Moet accompanies his handwritten note, including an invitation to do Shakespeare with him in England (my secret fantasy).[43]

The black-tie audience is wild as early as the overture. Rumors circulate of Paul Simon, Baryshnikov, Placido Domingo, Mayor Koch in the house. We're a huge hit. The aria tears the roof off. The entire house stands even before we begin the individual bows. An evening of total triumph. Praise Allah!

Backstage, I see all my beloved friends beaming as they climb the stairs, everyone with purple rose boutonnières. Mother's first words are, "I didn't know you were such an actor." I show off Napier's Growltiger costume sketch and the diamond-flecked locket from Andrew and Cameron. Sara and Edith, Aldyn, Jim Roman, Justin, Peter, Lenny, Sarah J. are all agog over the show and the unforeseen dimensions of my performance. At last they leave for Sardi's. I dress with Sara's help, don my party hair, and climb into the waiting limo that takes us to Sardi's and my parents on to Long Beach. At Sardi's, Aldyn is reading the *Times* review to hefty applause. I walk in, he skips to the paragraph about me, and the joint erupts into applause and a standing ovation. I soak it all in slowly, savoring this exquisite joy-laden moment. Subsequent ovations go to René Ceballos, Timmy, Ken Page, Betty, Donna, and more. It's divine. Howard and table toast

43 As of this writing still, alas, unachieved.

me with love. The *Times* review, despite intelligent reservations, is enthusiastic, and Betty and I get the burden of praise. Timmy is also well-received. I toast him as the greatest dancer on Broadway, and I meet his parents and Terry Cole Whittaker. The whole room is buzzing with our success. Utterly, utterly amazing. A dream.

Cameron rouses Jay and me with the *News* and *Post* reviews. Mixed, like the *Times*, but Clive Barnes calls me "fantastic" and "the best individual performance by far." The phone rings. Otis Bigelow says, "This is your friendly wake-up service. It's 12 o'clock and you're a star." More agents call: "Don't sign with anyone till you've talked to us." The *Wall Street Journal* devotes its first three paragraphs to Growltiger. So the day goes—unanimous raves for my performance, calls from friends, much well-wishing. Further congratulations at the theater and a deep moment with Tim, hurt and tearful, despite his best efforts to laugh off a bad notice in the *Post*. The *News* doesn't even mention him and it's all the fault of Gillie's refusal to tailor the dance to him (some of her press is unkind, as well). Trevor on the intercom tells us that despite the reviews the show "can't be stopped," the box office this morning took in $50,000 in the first 50 minutes and went on to set a world record of $250,000 in one day. Bernie Jacobs announces his conviction that we will run longer than *A Chorus Line*.[44]

The performance is anything but a second night slump. Gus gets a longer hand than ever, before the reprise. Is this the result of media-conditioned expectation? Time will tell. As I finish the reprise and turn to exit, some man in front house right emits a heartfelt, choked, "I love you, man," and the Bravos begin—first time ever at that moment. Wonderful, wonderful.

Sat 9 October Day 54

The matinee performance is wild, greatest house we've ever had. I rush out to pick up the rented car by 5:00 that will convey Jay and me up to the Berkshires for the day off. Then there's a meeting called at 6:45, for Trevor to make his farewell. The cast gathers in a tremulous and soul-filled mood. I'm crying before he even appears. He begins by talking about where the show goes from here. It must grow and change if it's to stay alive, yet fixed beats must remain and focus can't be diverted to down left when it should be up center. The ideology of development and spontaneity versus

[44] Sad to say, he did not live to see his prediction fulfilled on 19 June of 1997.

the reality of eight shows a week and set business and staging. What keeps us working in this art form that may become obsolete within our own lifetime. What is the nature of the contract that we renew nightly with every fresh audience and with each other. Our obligation to one another within the democratic context established from Day One. "If conflicts arise, don't hold them in and stew—talk to each other. The only theater I believe in is theater where people talk to each other." Everyone is sniffling and wiping their eyes. He celebrates our achievement, praises us as the most wonderful possible experience of an American company, and promises to return in January after *Peter Pan* opens at the RSC. "Speed the dawn," I exclaim, and we all line up for hugs. Tears stream down my face as we embrace. "I'll never be able to thank you enough," I sob, and he gulps in return. Then Betty, crying mightily, has her hug, and then "Timmie love." It's simply overwhelming. How profoundly and unalterably has this wonderful man touched all our lives. (In the wig room during prep, Betty and I still can't stop crying.) May it please God to keep him happy and well and serving the best in humanity through his work, and may we be reunited again and again in our work together, and our love for each other, through the joyful years to come.

EPILOGUE - 2001

The history of *Cats* subsequent to its Broadway opening is a
matter of not only public record but legend: the seven Tony
Awards, the chalking up of more than 1000 performances
per Tony, the box office receipts of a billion dollars plus. My
own tale is shorter and less bushy; forgive me for wagging it.
I was thirty-five when *Cats* opened on Broadway. I am now
inescapably middle-aged, and though I've continued to work
as an actor, I have yet to revisit that level of prominence.
It's spooky to contemplate my resemblance to Gus the
Theater Cat, looking back on "that moment of mystery when
I made history." Whether the kinship demonstrates the uni-
versality of T.S. Eliot's vision or a superb cosmic irony, I
can't help noticing that memory, besides giving *Cats* its hit
song, was one of its dominant themes, a theme given extra
resonance by the passage of eighteen years.

The art of enduring a long run is fierce and can be
acquired only on the job. I left *Cats* after performing it for
fifteen months, during which stint I suffered a hairline frac-
ture of my fifth metatarsal bone, when one of two stage-
hands helping me out of the Growltiger escape net swung me
too far out and my foot hit a 2-by-4 support strut. I crawled
out from under the receding hydraulics for the Gus return,
recalled the moment of mystery and limped off—though not
on the original Gus foot—to discover upon removing my

shoe a lump the size of an egg. I walked on crutches for ten days and was out of the show for a full three weeks, just after the first Thanksgiving at the Winter Garden.

(Here I must digress to relate that with the Stage Manager's consent, I spent a week of that healing in the warmer climate of Key West. Of course, I brought my concertina along, and on the first afternoon when I could manage the walk to Mallory Square discovered that large crowds gathered there for the hour before sunset and the waterfront buzzed with hippie craftsellers and entertainers. I couldn't allow such an opportunity to pass, and so returned the following afternoon with concertina in tow, put its carrying case on the ground before me and ran thru my old San Francisco street repertoire, naturally including "Funiculi Funicula," which had won Trevor and Andrew's favor at my first audition. I sang four or five tunes and as I was counting up the loot after the crowd had dispersed, an unforgettably gap-toothed young hippie came up to me and said, "Wow, man, you're great, you oughta be on Broadway." Immensely tickled that the Universe could actually have cooked up this moment, I looked him straight in the eye and said, "I am." He shook his head as if unable to absorb the reply, and walked off in silence.)

Back in the show, I never had another mishap, but after ten or eleven months I started to suffer boredom, which I've heard defined as hostility without enthusiasm. I had indeed been nominated for the Tony as Best Featured Actor in a

Musical (the award went to the venerable tap dancer Honi Coles, of *My One and Only*), and once the Tony frenzy was spent (Trevor and Gillian both returned to polish the show that spring), the continued run began to wax anticlimactic. I left at the beginning of 1984, the same night Donna King gave her final Bombalurina performance. I must pay tribute to the great Marlène Danielle who played *Cats* for the entire length of its run starting as a swing, and after covering several female roles, took over Bombalurina, which she sang and danced with electrifying verve right up thru her magnificent Closing Night performance. I could never have survived eighteen years of Growltiger, and not only for its physical demands. My journal has enabled me to relive giftlike moments such as "Growltiger getting religion and praying for forgiveness," or closing my eyes on "made history," but thrilling though such discoveries are, their repeated execution inevitably becomes a matter of routine. Joy in performance is a quality I cannot counterfeit, and once it goes, make-believe dwindles into pretense.

I told myself as much by writing, on Day 43 (Mon, 27 September), "it seems as if last week's four previews were a quirky experiment interrupting the rehearsal process." A journal of the run of *Cats* would have a very different tilt, lacking, of course, the central character. Trevor returned from time to time over the years, but he largely devoted himself to subsequent productions, on stage and film, that have continued to excite the world's imagination. I never did work with him again, though I played Thénardier in *Les Misérables* in London while he was preparing the American premiere in Washington and New York. Neither of us is too old to yet accompany one another on a Shakespeare expedition.

What he taught me about acting will never leave me. I'm so glad I chronicled the rehearsal process and can re-examine the basic truths of my profession after years peppered with perks as well as disappointments. When a talented and willing company meets a brilliant director, over time the process comes to exemplify all that is best in our species. The freedom to behave as if no one were looking is fused with scrupulous attention to that behavior's consequences; on the one hand complete self-consciousness and on the other, none. A living organism is built from powerful elements of cooperation, shared feeling, investigation, courage, and humor, in which the precise application of a huge range of personal skills reinforces the sense of community, spontaneity, and play. Not a bad way to run an enterprise, or a nation, or a planet!

Although AIDS is never once mentioned in this journal (its existence had become public knowledge about a year before rehearsals began), it eventually claimed several members of the company, including René Clemente, Reed Jones, and the surpassingly wonderful Timothy Scott, whose health and stamina problems during rehearsal were probably related to the virus, long before it was identified as HIV. Cameron Duncan, with whom I shared the loft downtown, was likewise taken, and too many others, known and unknown, not to mention those felled more predictably by the passage of time. Tyler Gatchell, the exemplary general manager who attributed his hassle-reducing style to the belief that "life is too short," died of a heart attack at age fifty en route to the London premiere of *Sunset Boulevard*. In view of such losses, fame for no sake but its own seems to matter so little. It is a strange profession where one's ego can get stroked for the skill one displays in submerging it. The life that theater seeks to illuminate rests upon ever-shifting foundations of achievement and regret. But the world turns forward only; the past recedes, the future approaches.

THE BALLAD OF MIGHTY MELVIN
or
ONE MAN LAUGHED

There was once a famous actor, Mighty Melvin was his name;
From Gibraltar to Samoa every tongue rang his acclaim.
He could wow them on a yacht and he could wow them on a
    raft,
But the night they all remembered was the Night That One
    Man Laughed.
'Twas a Xmas night performance, very gala, oh so posh;
There was caviar in the boxes, Quiche Lorraine, and succo-
    tosh;
They'd been standing since eleven and they would have
    called you daft
If you told them then they'd soon behold the Night That
    One Man Laughed.

As the evil Baron Malo Mighty Melvin swirled with pride,
'Twas the role that Barrymore bequeathed him (just before
    he died).
When he scowled, it was a laser; when he raged, it holo-
    graphed,
Even so it was remembered as the Night That One Man
    Laughed.
In a voice of pallid pleasure, and a robe of jet brocade
Malo told the fair Florinda that her lover had been spayed;
As he proffered her the poison, plus a stinging epitaph,
The satanic spell was broken by the sound of One Man's
    Laugh.

It was not a scornful snigger nor an extrovert guffaw
Nor a chortle nor a giggle but a gentle, mild, Haw, Haw.
"Who's that man?" the boxes bellowed, "Who's the disrespect-
    ful twerp
Who in Culture's very temple has the insolence to burp?"
As the curtain hurtled downward (for the drama was
    undone),

Mighty Melvin stepped before it and announced to everyone,
"Lovely ladies, worthy gentlemen, pray do not be distressed:
I know how to handle hecklers (bear in mind, I am the best).

"As our drama's brilliant climax has been utterly destroyed,
Let the culprit recompense us, let his penance fill the void.
Claim your punishment, offender, step before us like a man!"
And a voice from highest balcony said, "Catch me if you
      can."
In a flash, the tiny figure bolted up the neighboring aisle,
Then he shouted from the darkness in a voice that held a
      smile,
"You all take yourselves so serious, too serious by half,
So I thought I'd right the balance with the sound of One
      Man's Laugh."

"Seize that man," the standees shouted, while the boxes
      cried, "Gendarme,
Apprehend the boorish rascal, for we mean to do him harm."
Then from orchestra to rafters the whole audience, fore and
      aft,
Rose up, wrathful and indignant, to pursue the Man Who
      Laughed.
Down the polished marble stairways, over rugs of crimson
      plush
Swarmed a zealous, vengeful audience in a zealous, vengeful
      rush.
Knocking over crystal vases, spilling buckets of champagne,
Trampling antique Flemish tapestries, they scoured the place,
      in vain.

Mighty Melvin in his frenzy hurled his props to kingdom
      come
Then he tore his beard in tatters (heedless of the spirit
      gum).
He extinguished every footlight with a deadly train of kicks,
But what happened next convinced him that his ears were
      playing tricks:

From the fly-loft high above him, up where all the gaffers
gaffed,
Came the sound that tore the house down on the Night That
One Man Laughed.
"Haw Haw! Melvin you old hambone, don't you still remem-
ber me?
We wuz partners once in vaudeville," and the speaker shook
with glee.

Holding fast then to a fly rope, jumping sixty feet or more,
Counterweighted by a sandbag he descended to the floor.
"Well now, Mel, I guess your memory is only good for lines,
Though it's true that since we parted it's been thirty Auld
Lang Synes."
Mighty Melvin with amazement scanned the little fellow's
frame
Till the shock of recognition made him suddenly exclaim,
"Spelvin! Spelvin the Incredible! The Conjurer Supreme!
Is this one of your great magic feats, a riddle, or a dream?"

"It's all o' those," said Spelvin, slyly fondling his moustache,
"And it's also a reminder that you're full of balderdash.
Oh, I know you're rich and famous, but you used to be riff-
raff.
Do you think that I've forgotten how I once sawed you in
half?
Mighty Melvin, Mighty Melvin," (and he half choked back a
sob)
"Though you've gone from stooge to riches, do you have to
be a snob?
Though you play in fancy fol-de-rols for High Societee,
Do you think that makes you better than a theater rat like
me?"
Mighty Melvin's streak of sentiment quadrupled now in size.
"Oh, Spelvin, you're so right!" said he, and wiped his misty
eyes.
"The glamour that surrounds me has quite banished from
my mind
My long-forgotten origins, the humble, creepy kind.

My dear friend, let me embrace you, yes, and clutch you to
    my heart,
And let me thank you, *publicly,* for giving me my start."
At Melvin's word the curtain rose; the audience grew dumb
To behold their Mighty Melvin being buddies with a bum.

"Lovely ladies, worthy gentlemen," the words from Melvin
    rolled,
"Tonight I've learned that friendship is more precious fa-a-a-r
    than gold.
In younger, less imposing days, I worked in vaudeville;
'Twas a grimy, tacky theater, but it still gave me a thrill.
A magician there befriended me and urged me on my way,
Encouragement that made of me the man I am today.
I'd like to introduce the man who once sawed me in half:
Perhaps you'll recognize him by the sound of One Man's
    Laugh."

Right on cue, obliging Spelvin let a laugh burst from his
    throat;
In an instant Melvin joined him (on a somewhat deeper
    note).
The reason for the merriment was rather hard to tell,
But all at once the balcony began to laugh as well.
The contagious sound descended to the boxes and the pit,
Till in universal laughter all the audience was knit.
And to climax the ovation (everyone was cheering now),
Mighty Melvin and old Spelvin took their greatest, deepest
    bow.

.   .   .

Wall Street Journal, October 8, 1992
By Edwin Wilson

Tim* Webber Brings His Curious 'Cats' to Broadway

* The *Wall Street Journal* mistakenly printed "Tim" Webber instead of "Lloyd" Webber.

One of the high points of "Cats," the multi-million dollar musical that opened last night at the Winter Garden Theater, is "Growltiger's Last Stand." Growltiger is a ferocious cat — "the roughest cat that ever roamed at large" — who terrorizes all other cats.

The scene is played as a mock opera. Growltiger is aboard his pirate ship and in the distance, small, red-sailed sampans, bearing Siamese cats, come after him, bobbing through cardboard seas. But Growltiger (Stephen Hanan) does not see them coming; he is distracted by his lover Griddlebone (Bonnie Simmons), a feline femme fatale in white feathers and furs. While the two sing a comic operatic duet, the Siamese warriors sneak aboard the ship, capture Growltiger and make him walk the plank.

The number is wildly comic, with just the right amount of exaggeration. Would that the creators of "Cats" had understood the difference between the excesses required for a mock heroic scene such as this and the rest of the musical, but unfortunately they did not. There are many sensational numbers in the show, but hardly a one escapes overkill.

There was the danger of this from the start. "Cats" is based on T.S. Eliot's "Old Possum's Book of Practical Cats," a slim volume of poems Eliot wrote in the 1930s about all kinds of cats: mysterious cats, dramatic cats, fat cats. The poems were occasional pieces, written for Eliot's godchildren and friends, filled with whimsy and satire.

Composer Andrew Lloyd Webber had the novel and daring idea that the poems could make the basis for a musical. A man who is single-handedly establishing the British musical, Mr. Webber had previously written "Joseph and the Amazing Technicolor Dreamcoat," "Jesus Christ Superstar" and "Evita" with partner Tim Rice. For Eliot's verses he has composed an eclectic but engagingly tuneful score; he has the ability to create quiet, haunting melodies as in the song "Memory" and bouncy numbers about railway cars and midnight balls.

The original "Cats," directed by Trevor Nunn and choreographed by Gillian Lynne, became a solid hit in London where it is still playing. Not having seen that version, I cannot comment on how it was done. On Broadway, however, "Cats" has been given the full treatment: $4 million worth. Over a million has been spent on the

Winter Garden alone. Holes have been put through the roof and dug into the granite below the stage to accommodate special effects. Inside, the theater has been turned by designer John Napier into a vast junkyard. Old tires, broken tennis racquets, dirty paper plates, worn-out shoes—a collage of discarded items surrounds not only the stage but the sides of the boxes and balconies too. Moreover, all these items are made three times life-size so that they appear as they would to a cat. It is a triumph of pop sculpture worthy of the most far-out gallery in Soho.

Into this setting David Hersey had introduced enough lighting effects to make Con Edison turn handsprings. Strings of lights encircle the auditorium, flashing and blinking; washes of color move across the stage as if painted by a giant brush; bolts of lightning shoot from the sky. In the midst of all this, 30 lithe and limber performers cavort in clever cat costumes.

In the penultimate scene of the play a cat named Grizabella (Betty Buckley) climbs aboard a contraption resembling the spaceship that took E.T. home, and ascends into the heavens through that hole in the ceiling. It is a dazzling effect that leaves you breathless—until you begin wondering what this apotheosis has to do with the low-key lyrics of Eliot and the simple melodies of Mr. Webber. Not a great deal, I'm afraid.

The question is equally relevant to the staging of Mr. Nunn and choreography of Ms. Lynne. The best dance number in the show is "Mr. Mistoffolees," about a conjuring cat. In the title role Timothy Scott electrifies the audience with a series of spins and turns that build to a crescendo that seems a sure-fire finish. But the number is not over; it continues with an anti-climactic coda. The same thing happens time and again and one wonders why Mr. Nunn and Ms. Lynne cannot stop when they're ahead.

Sometimes there is an attempt to create something out of nothing. The big dance number near the end of act one, "The Jellicle Ball," goes on and on. Ms. Lynne's choreography becomes increasingly repetitious; the music swells, the lights change frantically—and it becomes obvious that all of this is done in an attempt to induce a climax where none exists.

The joys to be derived from a quieter moment—true to the spirit of the Eliot original—are illustrated in "Gus: the Theater Cat." Standing alone at center stage, Stephen Hanan plays an aging actor who glories in the theater the way it used to be. "These kittens," he observes, "do not get trained, as we did in the days when Victoria reigned."

"Cats" is an anomaly. The world it creates is refreshingly novel, its talented performers move with agility and grace and Mr. Webber has composed a score of eminently hummable tunes. In the second act, these are frequently combined to create spectacular scenes. The first act, however, is flat and overlong. And there remains that wide, sometimes unbridgeable gap between the magnitude of the production and Eliot's simple, charming lyrics. Like Rum Tum Tugger, one of the characters in the show, Mr. Webber's musical "is a curious cat."

The New Yorker October 11, 1982
By Brendan Gill

THE THEATRE: Homage to Cats

The setting of "Cats," at the Winter Garden, is a city dump of superlative squalid disorder, and it is there that the assortment of singing and dancing cats who make up the entire cast of this peculiar musical forgather by night to boast of their exploits, to contemplate old age and death, and, in one lucky instance, to be translated into cat heaven, where cats await without impatience rebirth into one or another of the nine lives to which, by common cat calculation, they are said to be entitled. The peculiarity of the musical lies in how little actually takes place during the course of quite a long evening; instead of a proper book, we have a setting to music, by Andrew Lloyd Webber, of a number of poems about cats by T.S. Eliot, most of which Eliot published just over forty years ago, in a droll little volume entitled "Old Possum's Book of Practical Cats." (Scholars may be able to tell me why Eliot chose to call himself Old Possum when he was neither old at the time nor especially possumlike in appearance—"raccoon" would have been more like it—and what the adjective "practical" may have meant to him in

such a context; save as killers of mice, cats are surely among the least practical of creatures.) Mr. Webber jauntily manifests his memory of many modes of music-making as he moves from scene to scene, which is to say from poem to poem; the titles of these I am reluctant to mention, lest they make the Anglican and Royalist Eliot sound too schoolmasterishly quaint for our robust American taste. His cats have names like Bustopher Jones and Rumpleteazer and Old Deuteronomy, but the names prove to be more bearable in song than they look in print and the cats themselves are far from being sissies; they have led hard lives, and each of them might well say, paraphrasing Whitman, "I was the cat, I suffer'd, I was there."

In writing light verse, Eliot was looking back to Lear and Carroll, but there is less deliberate nonsense in him than in his distinguished predecessors; a certain note of Eliotesque angst emerges from time to time, not unwelcomely. Trevor Nunn, the brilliant director of "Cats," has found in Old Possum hints of the author of the "Four Quartets;" Nunn has also written the lyrics for the most memorable song in the show, which is called "Memory" and was suggested by Eliot's "Rhapsody on a Windy Night." A lovely and touching song, "Memory" is sure to become a classic; so, perhaps, is a song about Gus, the theatre cat, who claims to have acted with Irving and Tree, and who "used to know seventy speeches by heart." I had never expected to encounter pathos in cats, whether in real life or in art, but Eliot-Webber-Nunn has mitigated to some extent and for the time being my hitherto harsh view of the species.

Judged as a spectacle instead of simply as a musical, "Cats" is a triumph, and for this, much of the credit must go to John Napier, who designed both the setting and the costumes. What a gorgeous dump he has created for Eliot's invincible army of cats to prowl upon and howl upon, and behind what splendidly brindled and whiskery pelts he has concealed his actors and actresses! Scarcely less important than the setting, which occupies not only the stage of the Winter Garden but much of the auditorium as well, is the strenuously acrobatic choreography, directed by Gillian Lynne. Miss Lynne has caused the young American cast to enter with seeming ease into what is essentially an English production; they perform with that combination of grace and energy which is indispensable to the musical form. The cast is too big to be individually named; letting a few stand for many, I single out praise for Stephen Hanan, as Gus; Betty Buckley, as Grizabella; and Ken Page, as Old Deuteronomy. Let me also praise the designer of the lighting, David Hersey, and the conductor of the orchestra, Stanley Lebowsky. "Cats" is reputed to have the largest advance sale of any musical in history—something over six million dollars. Old Possum was a devotee of musical theatre; he would have rejoiced to see his cats in glory on Broadway.

The New York Post, October 8, 1982
By Clive Barnes

The Most Long-Awaited Show Catapults onto the Stage "CATS"
It's quite a musical but hardly purr-fect

One thing is certain. The new Broadway musical *Cats,* which purred into what is left of the Winter Garden Theater last night, is a shattering triumph for two men: the director Trevor Nunn and the designer John Napier.

This British import does less well by two other men—the composer Andrew Lloyd Webber and the posthumous lyricist T.S. Eliot—and one woman: choreographer, Gillian Lynne.

But all of them—including Eliot's estate—can giggle rhapsodically all the way to prosperity, because *Cats* has already created so much interest that it will be a deserved box-office hit. It is a phenomenon in London. It will be a phenomenon in New York.

For audiences hungry for musicals and novelty, *Cats* is made to order. It has an intriguing amalgam of feline behavior, the snob appeal of Eliot's poetry (laced with a suggestion of his transcendental philosophy), lyrically undemanding music that sounds vaguely classical and sheer genius in its staging. Here is a potent theatrical cocktail.

The idea to create a musical from T.S. Eliot's 1939 collection of children's verse, *Old Possum's Book of Practical Cats,* originally belonged to Lloyd Webber—but somewhere along the way Nunn seems to have taken it for his own and shaped it to his will.

What Eliot himself would have thought of the idea—which has Eliot's widow's enthusiastic sanction—is anyone's guess. When Alan Rawsthorne once wrote a background score to the same poems, Eliot commented: "I like the idea that they are read *against* the musical background and not themselves set to music!

Well, they *are* set to music here. Also—and more so here than in last year's original London production—Eliot's radiantly childlike view of anthropomorphic cats has been "cutesified."

There is a certain macabre, Edward Lear-like quality to the poems, that this show-biz, environmentalized extravaganza studiously ignores. When it is not being charming it is being either sentimentally lachrymose or portentously philosophical.

Old Possum had nothing to do with the redemption in this musical. It was a *practical* book about how to look at cats with the eyes of a child and the wit and fancy of a poet.

Hence, very adroitly, keeping to the text but with a few interpolations from other Eliot poems, Lloyd Webber and Nunn have carved out a kind of linking theme—a Mary Magdalene concept of a whore's rebirth—that gives the musical a line and shape. It is clever for the theater but unfair to the essence of the poems.

Lloyd Webber's score is breathtakingly unoriginal yet superbly professional. Much of the lyrical passages (including the already famous song *Memory* which has provided a hit for Barbara Streisand) are to Puccini what Richard Addinsell's *Warsaw Concerto* was to Rachmaninov.

At times the score sounds remarkably like discarded passages from Puccini's *Turandot,* but the orchestration, fuller here than in London, by David Cullen and Lloyd Webber himself, is splendid, and the music is admirably hummable, even haunting. Ghosts often are.

But what sets the seal on the show's theatrical success is the mad authority of its staging. From the first glitter of cats-eyes in a darkened theater and the scamper of bodies around the auditorium, to the incredibly staged apotheosis when the alley cat ascends to cat-house heaven on a space machine that would have sent E.T. home happily, scarcely an error is permitted.

The theater is transformed. Napier has gutted it, removed its proscenium arch, re-arranged the seating and made the whole scene into a garbage heap surrounded by a cavern. But what a garbage heap and what a cavern—as strange and beautiful as Napier's cleverly and humanly feline costumes.

I don't think I have ever seen such decorative virtuosity on stage before. The stage is fringed with the detritus of civilization, from a broken-down car to a discarded flotsam of cartons, bottles and junk. The whole magic wasteland is scaled to the proportions of a cat.

The set is far more elaborate than in London—despite London's use of a revolving audience, planetarium-style—but one quibble: it seems strange to fill this rubbish heap with distinctly American junk that contrasts with the London topography and English sensibility of the text.

What Trevor Nunn has aimed for is the kind of lived-in naturalistic kind of behavior he captured in his *Nickolas Nickleby.* He gets it. These are cat people in a cat world, and despite all the tumultuous theatrical shocks and show-offs, most of them are piercingly enjoyable. It is the simplicity that gives Nunn's work its ultimate gleam.

Strangely enough, the dancing devised by Miss Lynne was conventionally indifferent in London and is conventionally indifferent here. It was claimed that it was going to be much improved, only the claim was a pious hope, a gleam of intention unfulfilled.

Also, to judge by advance publicity, the creative team was overwhelmed by Broadway's performing talent and the show was going to be much better performed.

Far from being better performed, in some instances the London cast was far preferable. Just as some of Lloyd Webber's changes —the new "Italian" aria in the pirate-king incident, for example— are mistakes, so is some of the casting.

Neither of the mistily wan Betty Buckley as the broken-hearted alley cat Grizabella nor Ken Page as the patriarchal Deuteronomy is a match for London's Elaine Page and Brian Blessed, while to compare the nonentity of Timothy Scott with the greatness of Wayne Sleep in the principal dancing role is merely to draw attention to the creative paucity of Miss Lynne's choreography.

Yet as an ensemble the American cast does work better than its British predecessor, and Stephen Hanan, whether cast as an epicure clubman, a theater cat or an amorous pirate, is fantastic. His is by far the best individual performance, with only a few others coming close.

But remember, *Cats* is more than the analysis of its parts. Its importance lies in its wholeheartedness. It is a statement of the musical theater that cannot be ignored, should prove controversial and will never be forgotten.

Thanks to Trevor Nunn and Napier—and to Lloyd Webber, who has enabled them to start their miracles—this is theatrical wizardry at a compromised level of genius. But a great show, in itself and by itself, not it isn't. Still, see it. Or at least see if you can get tickets for it.

The New York Times, October 8, 1982
By Frank Rich

Theater: Lloyd Webber's 'Cats'

There's a reason why "Cats," the British musical which opened at the Winter Garden last night, is likely to lurk around Broadway for a long time—and it may not be the one you expect.

It's not that this collection of anthropomorphic variety turns is a brilliant musical or that it powerfully stirs the emotions or that it has an idea in its head. Nor is the probable appeal of "Cats" a function of the publicity that has accompanied the show's every purr since it first stalked London 17 months ago. No, the reason why people will hunger to see "Cats" is far more simple and primal than that: it's a musical that transports the audience into a complete fantasy world that could only exist in the theater and yet, these days, only rarely does. Whatever the other failings and excesses, even banalities, of "Cats," it believes in purely theatrical magic, and on that faith it unquestionably delivers.

The principal conjurers of the show's spell are the composer Andrew Lloyd Webber, the director Trevor Nunn and the designer John Napier. Their source material is T.S. Eliot's one volume of light verse, "Old Possum's Book of Practical Cats." If the spirit of the Eliot poems is highly reminiscent of Edward Lear, the playful spirit of "Cats" is Lewis Carroll, refracted

through showbiz. Mr. Nunn and Mr. Napier in particular are determined to take us to a topsy-turvy foreign universe from the moment we enter the theater, and they are often more extravagantly successful at that here than they were in the West End "Cats" or in their collaboration on "Nicholas Nickleby."

Certainly the Winter Garden is unrecognizable to those who knew it when. To transform this house into a huge nocturnal junkyard for Eliot's flighty jellicle cats, Mr. Napier has obliterated the proscenium arch, lowered the ceiling and stage floor and filled every cranny of the place with a Red Grooms-esque collage of outsized rubbish (from old Red Seal records to squeezed-out toothpaste tubes) as seen from a cat's eye perspective. Well before the lights go down, one feels as if one has entered a mysterious spaceship on a journey through the stars to a cloud-streaked moon. And once the show begins in earnest, Mr. Napier keeps his Disneyland set popping until finally he and his equally gifted lighting designer, David Hersey, seem to take us through both the roof and back wall of the theater into an infinity beyond.

The cast completes the illusion. Luxuriantly outfitted in whiskers, electronically glowing eyes, masklike makeup and every variety of feline costume—all designed by Mr. Napier as well—a top-notch troupe of American singer-dancers quickly sends its fur flying in dozens of distinctive ways. It's the highest achievement of Mr. Nunn and his associate director-choreographer, Gillian Lynne, that they use movement to give each cat its own personality even as they knit the entire company into a cohesive animal kingdom. (At other, less exalted times, Mr. Nunn shamelessly recycles "Nickleby" business, as when he has the cast construct a train—last time it was a coach—out of found objects.)

The songs—and "Cats" is all songs—give each cat his or her voice. If there is a point to Eliot's catcycle, it is simply that "cats are much like you and me." As his verses (here sometimes garbled by amplification) personify all manner of cat, so do the tuneful melodies to which Mr. Lloyd Webber has set them. The songs are often pastiche, but cleverly and appropriately so, and, as always with this composer, they have been orchestrated to maximum effect. Among many others, the eclectic musical sources include swing (for the busy Gumbie cat), rock (the insolent Rum Tum Tugger), Richard Rodgers-style Orientalism (a pack of Siamese) and Henry Mancini's detective-movie themes (Macavity, the Napoleon of crime).

But while the songs are usually sweet and well sung, "Cats" as a whole sometimes curls up and takes a catnap, particularly in Act I. The stasis is not attributable to the music or the energetic cast, but to the entire show's lack of spine. While a musical isn't obligated to tell a story, it must have another form of propulsion (usually dance) if it chooses to do without one. As it happens, "Cats" does vaguely attempt a story, and it also aspires to become the very first British dance musical in the Broadway tradition. In neither effort does it succeed.

If you blink, you'll miss the plot, which was inspired by some unpublished Eliot material. At the beginning the deity-cat, Old Deuteronomy (an owlishly ethereal Ken Page), announces that one cat will be selected by night's end to go to cat heaven—"the heaviside layer"—and be reborn. Sure enough, the only obvious candidate for redemption is chosen at the climax, and while the audience goes wild when the lucky winner finally ascends, it's because of Mr. Napier's dazzling "Close Encounters" spaceship, not because we care about the outcome of the whodunit or about the accompanying comic-book spiritualism.

As for Miss Lynne's profuse choreography, its quantity and exuberance do not add up to quality. Though all the cat clawings and slitherings are wonderfully conceived and executed, such gestures sit on top of a repetitive array of jazz and ballet clichés, rhythmically punctuated by somersaults and leaps.

It's impossible not to notice the draggy passages in a long number like "The Jellicle Ball," or the missed opportunities elsewhere. To a tinkling new music-hall melody that Mr. Lloyd Webber has written for Mungojerrie and Rumpleteazer, Miss Lynne provides only standard strutting. The stealthy Macavity number looks like shopworn Bob Fosse, and the battle of the Pekes and the Pollicles in Act I could be an Ice Capades reject. For the conjuring cat, Mr. Mistoffelees, Miss Lynne's acrobatics never match the superhuman promise of either the lyrics or the outstanding soloist, Timothy Scott.

It's fortunate for "Cats" that Miss Lynne is often carried by the production design and, especially, by her New York cast. At the risk of neglecting a few worthy names, let me single out such additional kitties as Anna McNeely's jolly Jennyanydots, Donna King's sinuous Bombulurina, Bonnie Simmons' tart Griddlebone, Reed Jones's railroad-crazed Skimbleshanks and Harry Groener's plaintive Munkustrap. Aside from the dubious intermingling of British and American accents—which is not justified by the uniformly English references in the lyrics—the only real flaw in this large company is Terrence V. Mann's Rum Tum Tugger, who tries to imitate Mick Jagger's outlaw sexuality and misses by a wide mark.

By virtue of their songs, as well as their talent, there are two other performers who lend "Cats" the emotional pull it otherwise lacks. Stephen Hanan, singing Gus the Theater Cat to the show's most lilting melody, is a quivering bundle of nostalgia and dormant hamminess who touchingly springs back to life in an elaborate flashback sequence. (He also contributes a jolly cat about town, Bustopher Jones, earlier on.) To Betty Buckley falls the role of Grizabella the Glamour Cat and the task of singing "Memory," the Puccini-scented ballad whose lyrics were devised by Mr. Nunn from great noncat Eliot poems, notably "Rhapsody on a Windy Night." Not only does Miss Buckley's coursing delivery rattle the rafters, but in her ratty, prostitute-like furs and mane she is a poignant figure of down-and-out catwomanhood.

One wishes that "Cats" always had so much feeling to go with its most inventive stagecraft. One wishes, too, that we weren't sporadically jolted from Eliot's otherworldly catland to the vulgar precincts of the videogame arcade by the overdone lightning flashes and by the mezzanine-level television monitors that broadcast the image of the offstage orchestra conductor (the excellent Stanley Lebowsky). But maybe it's asking too much that this ambitious show lift the audience—or, for that matter, the modern musical—up to the sublime heaviside layer. What "Cats" does do is take us into a theater overflowing with wondrous spectacles—and that's an enchanting place to be.

...rehearsal at the _____ ___ ___
...ice to be away from the theatre. Hillie
...es some tightening of the _____ ¬º She
... the most incredible wo_____ &
... & on with unflagging _____ s
...lso seems to have regain_____ eve
... is quite buoyant. I'm _____ y &
...o the gym for a sauna, _____
...amazed to discover that I've gained 10
...bs since rehearsals began!

7 o'clock call at the theatre. I
can't really comprehend that we're performing again: somehow it seems as if
last week's 4 previews were a quirky
experiment interrupting the rehearsal
process. But no, we have an audience
& a good one, though the day off has
sapped my Growltiger stamina & the
number exhausts me as thoroughly as
last week - but I add some things at
the end, chiefly GT getting religion &
praying for forgiveness before his leap,
the last hokey touch, heartily endorsed
by Trevor. After the show Marilyn
Redfield, her mother & some friends